THE KINGFISHER
ILLUSTRATED
HORSE&PONY
ENCYCLOPEDIA

WRITTEN BY
Sandy Ransford

PHOTOGRAPHED BY
Bob Langrish

KINGFISHER

KINGFISHER

Kingfisher Publications Plc
New Penderel House
283–288 High Holborn
London WC1V 7HZ

www.kingfisherpub.com

First published by Kingfisher Publications Plc 2004

3 5 7 9 10 8 6 4 2

AMS/0405/PROSP/CLSN(CLSN)/157MA/C

A CIP catalogue record for this book is available from the British Library.

ISBN 13: 978 0 7534 0969 5
ISBN 10: 0 7534 0969 0

FOR KINGFISHER
Publishing manager: Melissa Fairley
Art director: Mike Davis
Picture manager: Cee Weston-Baker
Production controller: Debbie Otter
DTP co-ordinator: Sarah Pfitzner
Artwork archivists: Wendy Allison, Jenny Lord
Proofreader: Sheila Clewley

PROJECT TEAM
Project director: Julian Holland
Designers: Marcus Andrews, Nigel White
Photographer: Bob Langrish

Printed in China

Contents

4   **Introducing the horse**
6   Natural world of horses
8   Life cycle of the horse
10 Domestication of the horse
12 Types of horse
14 Points of a horse
16 Colours
18 Markings
20 **What is a breed?**
22 **Hotblood horses**
24 Arab
26 Thoroughbred
28 Anglo-Arab, Barb, Akhal-Teké
30 **Coldblood horses**
31 Ardennais, Boulonnais
32 Percheron, Suffolk
34 Shire, Clydesdale
36 Brabant, Noriker, Friesian, Dutch Draught

38 **Warmblood horses**
39 Swedish Warmblood, Selle Français
40 Competition breeds
42 Oldenburg, Gelderlander, French Trotter, Camargue
44 Przewalski's Horse, Tarpan
46 Irish Draught, Hackney Horse, Cleveland Bay
48 Andalucian, Lusitano, Lipizzaner
50 Morgan, Criollo, Quarter Horse
52 Pinto, Palomino, Appaloosa
54 Tennessee Walking Horse, American Saddlebred, Missouri Foxtrotter, Standardbred
56 Mustang, Waler

57 Pony breeds
58 Dartmoor, Exmoor,
 Connemara, New Forest
60 Welsh Section A, B, C and D
62 Fell, Dales, Highland
64 Fjord, Icelandic, Haflinger
66 New breeds of the USA
68 Caspian, Chincoteague and
 Assateague, Basuto, Boer
70 Australian, Falabella, Shetland,
 Hackney
72 Keeping a pony
73 Providing company
74 What a pony needs
76 Ways to keep a pony
78 Where to keep a pony
80 A stable of your own
82 Stable management
84 Choosing a field
86 Looking after
 a pony's field
88 Turning out and
 catching
90 Feeding a pony
91 The rules of feeding
92 Different types of feed
94 A diet for your pony
96 Grooming a pony
97 Grooming equipment
98 Grooming routines
100 Feet and foot care
102 Washing a pony
104 Clipping a pony
106 Choosing a rug

108 Other care routines
109 Care after exercise
110 Shoeing a pony
112 Travelling safely
114 Summer and
 winter care
116 Health care
117 Signs of good health
118 Health routine
120 First aid
122 Common ailments
124 Caring for a sick pony

126 Before you start
127 Why have riding lessons?
128 Where to have
 riding lessons
130 Clothes to wear
 for riding
132 Types of pony
134 A pony's tack
135 Saddles and girths
136 Bridles and bits
138 Western tack
140 Fitting and caring for tack
142 Saddling up
144 Putting on a bridle
146 First lessons
147 Meeting your pony
148 Getting to know a pony
150 Mounting
152 Dismounting
154 How to sit in the saddle
156 The aids
158 On the lunge or leading rein
160 On your own
162 Turning left and right
164 Learning to trot
166 Canter on
168 Riding at top speed
170 Western riding

172 In the school
173 Riding in a group
174 Exercises in the school
176 Without stirrups and reins
178 Exercises in the saddle
180 Looking forwards
181 Road safety
182 Riding out
184 Your first
 jumping lessons
186 Jumping higher
188 Schooling steps
190 Advanced riding
192 Taking part in events
194 Getting ready
 for the show
196 Going to a show
198 Fun and games
200 Showjumping classes
202 Showing and
 dressage tests
204 Cross-country
206 Training and driving
208 Breaking in a horse
210 How to drive a horse
212 Harness and vehicles
214 Specially trained horses
216 Glossary
220 Index
224 Websites and
 acknowledgements

Introducing the horse

Przewalski's Horse
This horse, which was discovered living wild in Mongolia in the 1870s, looks very like the primitive ancestors of today's horses and ponies.

Generous, willing and patient, horses have served people well for thousands of years. We have ridden them, driven them, used them to pull heavy loads and to plough our fields, and fought battles from their backs. Immensely strong, yet very gentle, they look to us for leadership, which is why they allow us to tell them what to do. For centuries they were our only form of transport. Now we use horses and ponies mainly for pleasure, we owe it to them to learn as much as we can about them, to try to understand them, and to treat them kindly.

Domestication and training

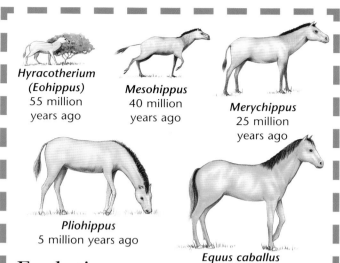

Hyracotherium (Eohippus)
55 million years ago

Mesohippus
40 million years ago

Merychippus
25 million years ago

Pliohippus
5 million years ago

Equus caballus
1.5 million years ago

Evolution

The earliest definite ancestor of the horse lived around 55 million years ago in North America. About as big as a fox, it had four toes on its front feet and three on its hind, and lived in marshy areas where it browsed on vegetation. Over the millennia, the horse got larger and its extra toes disappeared. Its teeth adapted to grazing, and the position of its eyes changed to give it all-round vision.

The horse has come a long way since its wild ancestry. A dressage horse, for example, is trained to obey the slightest movement of its rider's hands, legs and weight. An event horse is encouraged by its rider to clear fences it would never tackle on its own. A police horse will move towards a noisy and unruly crowd. A knowledgeable and sympathetic rider can calm a horse's fears, and prevent it from obeying its instinct to run from danger.

Wild ponies on Exmoor
Ponies and horses naturally live in family groups – mares, foals and young animals – with the herd stallion. Being on their own is unnatural, and makes them nervous.

In the show ring
The horse is such a remarkable animal that it can be trained to excel in a wide range of activities, like this beautifully turned out show horse.

Natural world of horses

Horses and ponies are herd animals. They form small groups, and within the groups, there are particular friendships and sometimes dislikes. In the wild, horses spend up to 20 hours a day grazing, constantly moving slowly to find food. When they rest, at least one group member stands guard over their sleeping companions.

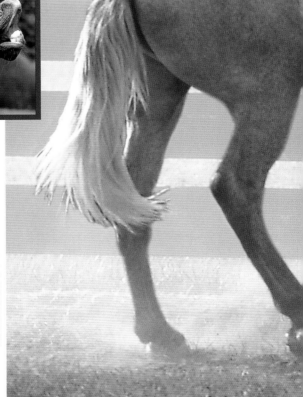

Domesticated horses

A pony can feel unhappy if he is kept on his own. If there are no other horses or ponies around, other animals, like sheep and cows, make quite good company. The life of a domesticated pony is not natural, so try to give your pony as much freedom as possible.

Mutual grooming

Wild and domesticated ponies often groom each other if they are friends. They scratch each other's neck, withers or back with their front teeth. This is their way of strengthening a friendship.

Flehmen reaction

A pony may curl up his top lip when he senses an unusual smell or taste. This curious action lets him draw air over a special sense organ in the roof of his mouth so that he can analyse the smell.

A horse's body language

Ears pricked forwards show that a horse is interested in what is going on, and expects good things to happen.

One ear to the side shows that the pony is distracted by something other than his main object of interest.

Ears laid back show anger or fear. The pony is warning you, or another pony, that he may kick or bite.

Herd animals

In the wild, horses and ponies, such as these mustangs in the USA, live in small family groups. These consist of one stallion, a few mares and their foals, and young animals that stay until they form herds of their own.

Fighting talk

In a group of horses and ponies, each animal has a position in a hierarchy, and squabbles occur if one horse tries to challenge for a higher position. In the wild, stallions fight off rivals, biting and striking out with a foreleg, or swinging their quarters round ready to kick. But horses and ponies threaten each other much more than they actually fight. Ears laid back and an outstretched neck are often enough to see off another pony.

A horse's age

You can tell how old a horse is by looking at its teeth. As it ages, its incisors, or front teeth, slope more, and their surface markings change.

A horse's age

You can tell how old a horse is by looking at its teeth. As it ages, its incisors, or front teeth, slope more, and their surface markings change.

Up to six months

Two years

Three years

Five years

Seven years

Nine years

15 years

25 years

Life cycle of the horse

Horses and ponies can continue growing until they are five or six years old, when they are mature. Before that, their bones are not strong enough for hard work. As they grow older, the shape of their teeth and the markings on them change. Horses are considered old from their late teens, but many continue to work happily into their twenties. They may live for 30 years or so.

In-foal mare

'In foal' means that a mare is pregnant. She carries her foal for 11 months, and towards the end of this time she looks very round. Her shape is especially noticeable from the front and back.

Newborn foal

When the foal is born, the mare licks it clean. It usually gets to its feet within an hour or so, when it will take its first drink of milk. Although they are wobbly at first, foals born in the wild can walk, trot and even gallop alongside their mothers a few hours after their birth.

Early days

For the first 12 months of its life, a horse or pony is called a foal. Long legs enable foals to move quickly. Foals suckle until they are four to six months old, but long before that start nibbling grass.

Yearling

Long-legged and gangling, a yearling is between 12 and 24 months old.

Two-year-old

By two, it begins to look like an adult, though it is still immature.

Four-year-old

At four a horse is almost mature, and is ready to begin its working life.

Ten-year-old

Between about five and 12 years old, a horse is in its prime. Horses that compete are at their peak during these years.

Old horse

Around 20 years old, there may be dips in its back and in front of its withers. Its legs and joints may become thickened.

Domestication of the horse

Early humans hunted horses for food. Around 6,000 years ago, they began to herd them, and may also have ridden them. Fossilized teeth seem to show that horses had bits in their mouths 500 years before the invention of the wheel. Horse-drawn chariots were used in war, and for racing and hunting wild animals. Cavalry gradually replaced the charioteers, and started the tradition of handling horses from their left sides. Whether ridden or driven, horses became vital for transport and work on the farm. It is only recently that we have used them mainly for recreation and pleasure.

Chariot racing

Chariot racing was a popular sport among the aristocracy in Roman times. This stone relief shows a team of horses racing in the Circus Maximus in Rome, and dates from the 2nd century.

Cave paintings

At Altamira, in northern Spain, horses are among the animals which appear in cave paintings that date back to between 15000 and 10000BCE.

Jousting

Medieval knights fought battles on horseback, and practised their skills in jousting tournaments. They charged at each other with raised lances, each aiming to knock the other off his horse.

Transport

The picture below shows the Duke of Beaufort's mail coach setting out from Piccadilly, London, in 1841. Passengers on mail coaches paid five old pence a mile for an inside seat and two-and-a-half old pence a mile for a seat on the top.

Napoleon

Because soldiers, including Napoleon, carried swords on the left, they had to mount from this side. They handled their horses from the left, and we still follow the tradition today.

High school

This horse is performing an artificial pace called the Spanish trot. Its forelegs are lifted very high and stretched out straight in front.

Types of horse

Horses and ponies vary in type from the large, heavily built, slow-moving draught horse to the slender, fast Thoroughbred; from the solid, weight-carrying cob to the elegant show pony. Types are usually a mixture of different breeds, though many are specially bred. For example, a heavy horse crossed with a Thoroughbred will produce a horse capable of carrying a large, heavy rider.

Driving types

Horses and ponies suitable for driving tend to have straight shoulders – on which the collar of the harness fits well – and upright pasterns. They often have high action, which looks good when they are pulling a carriage, but would be very uncomfortable in a riding horse.

Heavy horses
This type of horse is massively built. Their bones are huge and they have enormous muscles. They are capable of pulling very heavy weights.

Carriage horses
These types must also be strong, but they are lighter, more elegantly built, and often high-stepping. A matching pair is highly prized.

Riding types

A riding horse or pony has to be strong enough to carry its rider, but narrow enough to ride. Sloping shoulders give a horse a long, low stride, which is comfortable to sit to. Sloping pasterns also make a horse a good ride, while powerful hindquarters and long hind legs give jumping ability.

Show pony
A show pony or the larger version, called a show hack, has all the best points of a riding pony or horse. It must be beautiful, have good conformation and paces, and behave perfectly.

Cob
A cob is a quiet riding horse, with short legs and a deep body. Traditionally it was ridden by elderly, often heavy, riders. A cob's mane is usually hogged.

Polo ponies
These are actually small horses. They have to be fast, able to start, stop and turn quickly, and must obey their riders' commands instantly.

Working hunter pony
This is more solidly built and plainer than the classic show pony. As well as being a good general riding pony, it must be able to gallop and jump.

Points of a horse

The points of a horse or pony are the visible parts of his anatomy. Each has a name, which you will find useful to learn, as they will help you understand magazines and books you read, and instructions you may be given when you take riding lessons. By becoming familiar with these terms you will learn more about horses and ponies, and be better able to talk to other people interested in horses. You will be able to discuss pony care, and talk over any problems with a vet.

Conformation

Conformation means the way in which a horse or pony is put together. It varies according to type and breed, but the body should look in proportion. A small head; large, clear eyes; sloping shoulders and pasterns; a good circumference of bone below the knee; a short back and powerful hindquarters are considered good conformation.

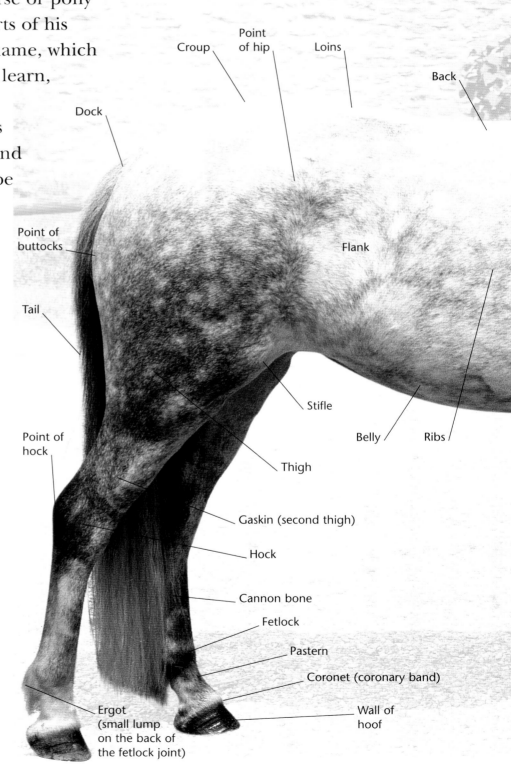

Croup
Point of hip
Loins
Back
Dock
Point of buttocks
Flank
Tail
Stifle
Belly
Ribs
Point of hock
Thigh
Gaskin (second thigh)
Hock
Cannon bone
Fetlock
Pastern
Coronet (coronary band)
Ergot (small lump on the back of the fetlock joint)
Wall of hoof

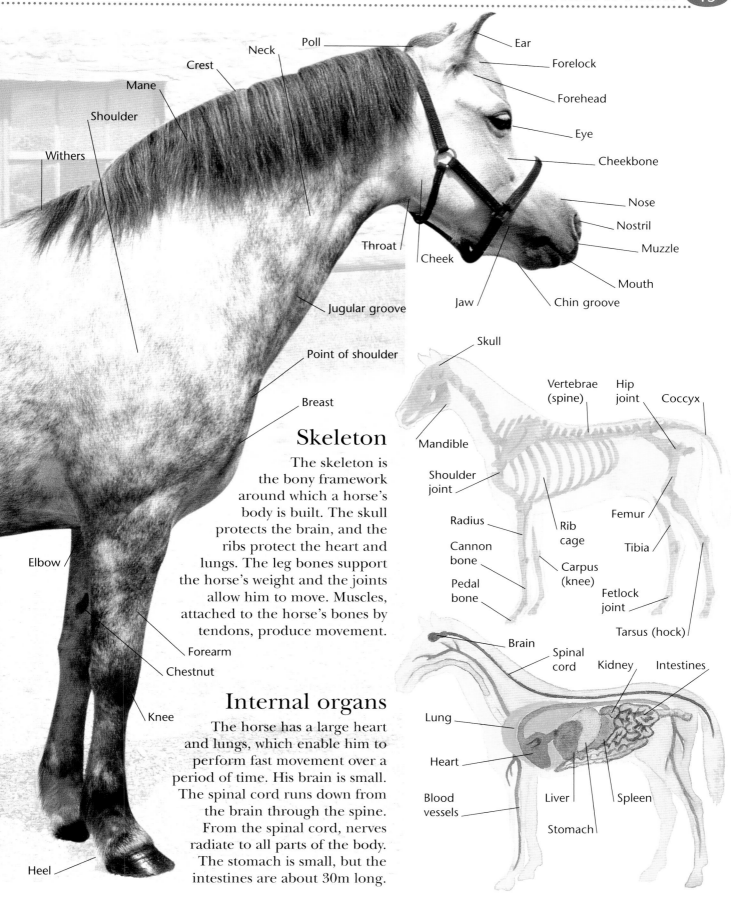

Poll

Neck

Crest

Mane

Shoulder

Withers

Ear

Forelock

Forehead

Eye

Cheekbone

Nose

Nostril

Muzzle

Throat

Cheek

Mouth

Jaw

Chin groove

Jugular groove

Point of shoulder

Breast

Skeleton

The skeleton is the bony framework around which a horse's body is built. The skull protects the brain, and the ribs protect the heart and lungs. The leg bones support the horse's weight and the joints allow him to move. Muscles, attached to the horse's bones by tendons, produce movement.

Elbow

Forearm

Chestnut

Knee

Heel

Skull

Mandible

Shoulder joint

Radius

Cannon bone

Pedal bone

Vertebrae (spine)

Hip joint

Coccyx

Femur

Tibia

Rib cage

Carpus (knee)

Fetlock joint

Tarsus (hock)

Internal organs

The horse has a large heart and lungs, which enable him to perform fast movement over a period of time. His brain is small. The spinal cord runs down from the brain through the spine. From the spinal cord, nerves radiate to all parts of the body. The stomach is small, but the intestines are about 30m long.

Brain

Spinal cord

Kidney

Intestines

Lung

Heart

Blood vessels

Liver

Spleen

Stomach

Colours

The colour of a horse's or pony's coat depends on the amount of pigment, or natural colouring, in its skin. Almost all horses and ponies have dark skin, except where they have white markings, such as on the face and lower legs, where the skin is pink. Only rare, pure-white horses called albinos have pink skin all over. Most horses and ponies that we think of as white are actually grey. They have dark skin, which you can see on their muzzles.

As horses age

As horses and ponies grow older, their colour may change. Greys are born dark and gradually become lighter, until they look white. Some greys develop dark, usually brown, flecks. This colour is called 'flea-bitten grey'. Browns, blacks, bays and chestnuts may have some white hairs in their coats, manes and tails.

Bay is a rich, reddish-brown coat colour with black mane, tail and lower legs.

Flea-bitten grey is a light grey colour with dark, usually brown, flecks.

Bright bay is lighter than bay, with more yellow in the coat colour.

Brown is dark brown, often with paler areas. Also called dark bay.

Dapple grey has black and white hairs that form rings called dapples.

Black is black all over, including the mane and tail. Pure black is rare.

Eye colour

The colour of a horse's or pony's eyes, like that of its coat, is decided by the amount of pigment it has. As most horses and ponies have dark skin, so most also have brown eyes. But occasionally, as with the albino, and sometimes with spotted horses, the eyes are light coloured. In the Appaloosa breed, the white of the eye can be seen all the time.

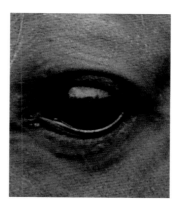 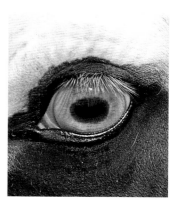

Brown eyes
The iris of the eye is dark brown. The white of the eye, which surrounds the iris, can be seen only when the horse is frightened or angry.

Wall eyes
In a wall eye, the iris is bluish- or pinkish-white. This unusual colour does not affect the horse's sight. These are also called china, blue or glass eyes.

Hoof colour

The colour of the horn of a horse's or pony's hooves is related to the colour of its coat on the leg just above the hoof. Black or dark-coloured legs have dark hooves, which are called blue. Where there are white socks or other leg markings, the hooves are light-coloured, and are called white. A horse may have hooves that are different colours.

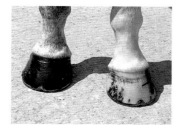 

Blue hoof and white hoof
The pony's leg shown on the left of the picture is dark and has a blue hoof. The leg on the right has a white sock, so the hoof is also white.

Striped hooves
Horse and pony breeds with spotted coats, such as the Appaloosa, have striped hooves (above). Light and dark stripes run up and down the feet.

Liver chestnut is a darker chestnut, like the colour of raw liver.

Chestnut is red-gold or ginger, often with darker or lighter mane and tail.

Blue roan is black with white growing through it, giving a bluish colour.

Strawberry roan is chestnut with white hairs growing through it.

Yellow dun is a yellowish, biscuit-coloured coat with black points.

Skewbald is brown and white patches all over. Also called part-coloured.

Piebald is black and white patches all over. Also called part-coloured.

Spotted is dark spots on a white coat or white spots on a dark coat.

Markings

The word 'markings' means all the patches and stripes on a horse or pony that are a different colour from its coat. These markings are usually white and appear on the face and legs. The shape and size of the markings varies a lot between different horses, and they are recorded, and used to help to identify the animal.

Face markings

Marks on the face are white and usually appear on the front of the face. These marks may cover a large area or a very small one, and can be of many different shapes. To make it easier to describe these marks and record them, different types of markings are given special names.

Blaze is a fairly broad white band down the face.

Flesh marks

White patches on the underside of a horse's belly and on its flanks are called 'flesh marks'. These marks are often seen on Clydesdale horses (left). Sometimes, horses have white marks on their backs or in other places. These are usually the result of an injury or wound, and are called 'acquired marks'.

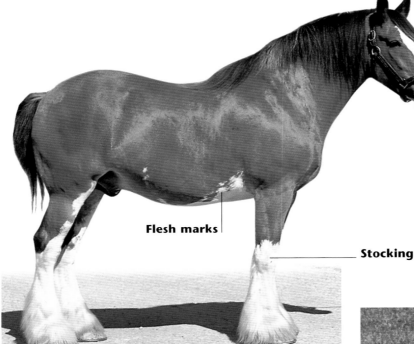

Blaze

Flesh marks

Stocking

Leg markings

Leg markings are mostly white and are usually called socks or stockings, but there may also be dark marks. When markings are written down to help to identify a horse, they are described very carefully. For example, a certificate may say 'white mid-pastern to coronet' or 'white to mid-cannon'.

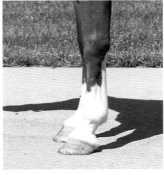

Socks are white marks that go above the fetlock but not as far as the knee or hock.

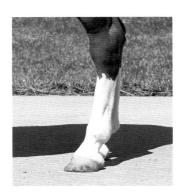

Stockings are white marks that reach and sometimes cover the knee or hock.

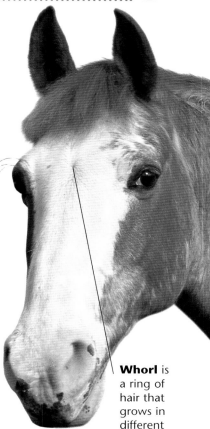

Stripe is a narrow band of white down the face.

Star is a white mark of any shape on the forehead.

Snip is a patch of white on the nose between the nostrils.

Whorl is a ring of hair that grows in different directions.

Eel stripe

Primitive breeds, such as Przewalski's Horse (right), and Fjord and Highland ponies often have a black stripe running along their backs from the mane to the tail. This is called an 'eel' or 'dorsal' stripe, and is usually seen with a dun-coloured coat.

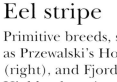

Eel stripe

White face

A very broad white blaze that goes all the way across the front of a horse's face is called a 'white face'. It reaches as far as the eyes and covers the horse's muzzle.

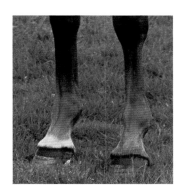

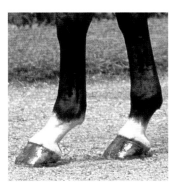

White coronets cover the area just above the hoof, which is called the coronet.

White pasterns cover the pastern area between the hoof and the fetlock joint.

Ermine marks are small dark spots on white socks next to dark marks on the hooves.

Zebra marks are horizontal dark stripes on the lower legs seen in ancient breeds.

What is a breed?

Horses and ponies vary in shape and size. Some belong to a particular breed. This means that they share the same characteristics as other horses or ponies of the same breed. Horse breeds are divided into groups called coldblood, hotblood and warmblood. The pony breeds are not usually classified in this way.

Coldbloods

Brabants (above) are typical coldblood horses. Coldbloods come from northern Europe, where the cool, damp weather produces plenty of rich grazing. This makes the horses bred there large and very strong.

Warmbloods

Warmblood breeds were produced by crossing hotbloods and coldbloods. This horse (left) is a warmblood, although it does not belong to a specific breed. It is a 'type' called a heavyweight hunter. Types of horse are defined by the kind of work they do.

Hotbloods

The Anglo-Arab (above) is a fine example of the beauty, grace and elegance of the hotblood breeds. Hotbloods originally came from the Middle East and North Africa, where poor grazing and the extreme climate produced a light, tough, fast horse.

Ponies

Ponies stand up to 14.2hh (147cm) and most, like the Icelandics (right), are warmbloods. Ponies have shorter legs than horses, and they are stronger in relation to their size. They are sturdy, tough and independent.

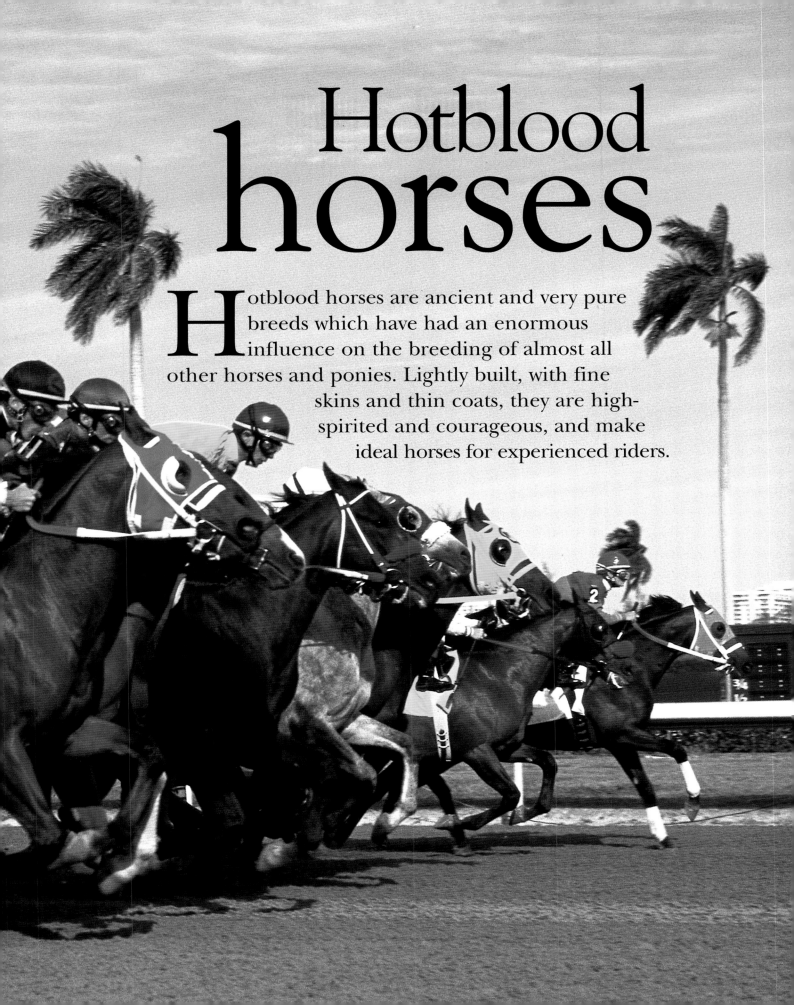

Hotblood
horses

Hotblood horses are ancient and very pure breeds which have had an enormous influence on the breeding of almost all other horses and ponies. Lightly built, with fine skins and thin coats, they are high-spirited and courageous, and make ideal horses for experienced riders.

Arab

The Arab is probably the oldest and most beautiful breed of horse in the world. It has played an important part in the development of horse and pony breeds in almost every country. With its high head and tail carriage, great 'presence' and floating action, an Arabian horse is instantly recognizable. Although it is a small horse, the Arab is strong, and famous for its stamina.

Arabian head

The head is small and elegant, with a 'dished', or concave, profile. The neck has a high crest. The angle at which the neck joins the head, called the *mitbah*, is seen only in this breed.

An Arab's back is short and compact because it has fewer bones in its spine than other horses. The joints of the legs are flat and the pasterns are sloping. The chest is broad, and the feet are hard and well-formed.

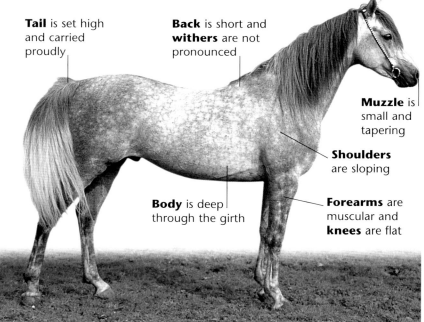

Tail is set high and carried proudly

Back is short and **withers** are not pronounced

Muzzle is small and tapering

Shoulders are sloping

Body is deep through the girth

Forearms are muscular and **knees** are flat

Mare and foal
An Arabian horse is high-spirited and courageous, but it also has a kind and gentle nature which makes it easy to handle. Arab foals are lively and inquisitive.

Desert horses

Arabs were first bred in the deserts of the Arabian peninsula, where they have existed for at least 4,000 years. Poor food and harsh conditions have produced a small, fast horse that is strong and tough. They were raced over more than 450km, and regarded as prized possessions by their owners.

Facts and figures

- **Place of origin**
  The Arabian peninsula,
  now called Saudi Arabia

- **Height**
  14.2–15hh (147–152cm),
  or larger

- **Colour**
  Mostly chestnut, bay and
  grey; brown and black
  are seen rarely

- **Uses**
  General riding; showing;
  endurance riding;
  specialist racing; also as a
  cross with other breeds
  to produce quality show
  hacks and ponies

- **Characteristics**
  Courageous and gentle

Thoroughbred

The Thoroughbred is the fastest breed of horse in the world. It was produced in England in the 17th and 18th centuries by crossing three Arab stallions – the Darley Arabian, the Godolphin Arabian and the Byerley Turk – with English mares. Thoroughbreds have developed into perfect racehorses. They have also had a huge effect on horse breeding throughout the world. They succeed at all kinds of equestrian sports, and make good riding horses.

Thoroughbred breeding

Thoroughbred horses are very valuable. Those to be used for racing are called bloodstock, and are bred from former racehorses on special stud farms. Young horses are turned out together in paddocks until they are old enough to begin their training.

On the gallops

When Thoroughbred racehorses have become used to carrying a rider and obeying commands, they are trained on stretches of land called gallops. Here they can gallop for long distances. They usually exercise in groups, called strings, supervised by their trainers.

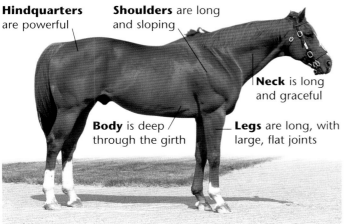

Hindquarters are powerful

Shoulders are long and sloping

Neck is long and graceful

Body is deep through the girth

Legs are long, with large, flat joints

Steeplechasing

Thoroughbreds compete in both flat racing and racing over fences, which is called 'steeplechasing'. The grey above right is Desert Orchid, one of the most successful of recent steeplechasers. He is shown here racing at Cheltenham, England, in 1990.

Eventing
Many horses that compete in eventing are either pure- or part-bred Thoroughbreds.

Many people believe that this breed is the perfect riding horse. Its sloping shoulders and long pasterns produce long, low strides, making it comfortable to ride. Its powerful quarters give it great speed. It is light and graceful, yet strong, and has great stamina.

Facts and figures

- **Place of origin**
  England

- **Height**
  15.2–16.2hh
  (157–168cm)

- **Colour**
  Brown, bay,
  chestnut, grey
  Always solid colours

- **Uses**
  Racing; riding;
  showing; dressage;
  showjumping;
  eventing

- **Characteristics**
  Fast, courageous,
  but also highly
  strung and can be
  difficult to handle

Anglo-Arab

The Anglo-Arab is a cross between the Arab and the Thoroughbred. It has the beauty and intelligence of the Arab, and the size and speed of the Thoroughbred. Although the breed originated in England, much of its development took place in France.

Withers are higher than Arab's

Quarters are strong

Head has Arab's gentle expression

Legs have plenty of bone

Body is deep through the girth

Endurance riding

Anglo-Arabs, as well as pure-bred and part-bred Arabs, compete very successfully in long-distance endurance rides. The horses must be extremely fit and have great stamina, as they may have to travel up to 80km a day at an average speed of 14–15km/h. Some endurance rides last for more than one day.

The head is straighter in profile than the Arab's, and the horse looks more like a Thoroughbred because of its greater size. Its long legs enable it to move with great speed. Its size means that it does very well in eventing and showjumping, as well as in dressage.

Key facts

- **Height**
  15.2–16.2hh
  (157–168cm)

- **Colour**
  Bay, chestnut, brown, grey

- **Uses**
  Riding; endurance; dressage; showjumping

Barb

The Barb comes from Morocco, in North Africa, and is one of the world's oldest breeds. Although it is not beautiful, the Barb is sound and tough, and has great stamina. It is capable of great speed over short distances.

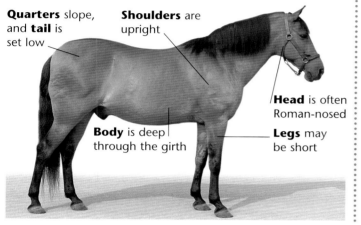

Quarters slope, and **tail** is set low

Shoulders are upright

Head is often Roman-nosed

Body is deep through the girth

Legs may be short

Head shape

The Barb is such an ancient breed that its skull shape is similar to that of primitive horses. The head is quite large and plain and does not have the Arab's grace and beauty.

The Barb, like the Arab, has had a great influence on horse breeding throughout the world. The Spanish Horse, from which many horse and pony breeds were developed, was itself descended from the Barb. The breed is the traditional mount of the Berbers of North Africa.

Mane and **tail** are thick and full

Akhal-Teké

Bred in the deserts of Turkmenistan, north of Iran, the Akhal-Teké is an unusual-looking horse. It has a long, lean body and neck, and long legs. It is capable of great feats of endurance, and is used for long-distance riding, racing, jumping and dressage.

The Akhal-Teké has been bred for thousands of years. It is spirited and courageous, hardy and strong. This breed stands about 15.2hh (157cm) and has a fine coat and a silky mane and tail. The most prized colour is this unique metallic golden dun.

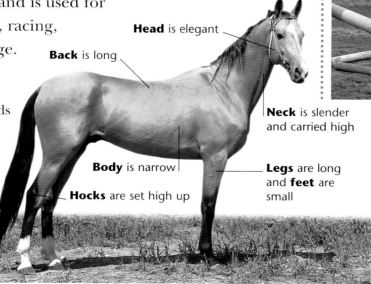

Head is elegant

Back is long

Body is narrow

Hocks are set high up

Neck is slender and carried high

Legs are long and **feet** are small

Good jumper

Because of its great stamina, the Akhal-Teké is mainly known for its success in long-distance riding and racing. But it is also a good jumper, and competes successfully in both showjumping and dressage.

Coldblood horses

Coldblood breeds are large, heavy and very strong. Many have existed for thousands of years. They were bred for farm work and for pulling heavy loads. Coldbloods have calm and docile natures. Most have 'feather' – hair – round their feet.

Ardennais

This heavy draught horse has been bred in the Ardennes region, on the borders of France and Belgium, for hundreds of years. It is probably descended from medieval warhorses. In the 19th century, the Ardennais developed into two main types – a massive farm horse and a more lightweight animal.

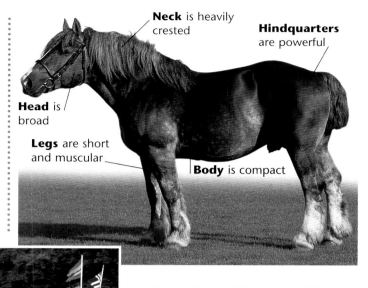

Neck is heavily crested

Hindquarters are powerful

Head is broad

Legs are short and muscular

Body is compact

Crowd-pullers

Ardennais are not often used for farming today, but these good-natured, easy-to-handle horses are still popular at shows. This pair, pulling a farm wagon, are the typical red roan colour.

Ardennais stand between 15 and 16hh (152–163cm). They are tough, hardy animals, able to withstand a harsh climate and do well on poor food. Ardennais horses are often roan in colour, although they may also be bay, chestnut or grey.

Hindquarters are very muscular

Neck has a massive crest and a fine, silky mane

Head is elegant

Shoulders are powerful

Legs are huge and carry little feather

Despite its size, the Boulonnais is an elegant horse due to its Arab and Barb ancestors. It is usually grey, but also sometimes black, roan, bay or chestnut. This horse is well proportioned, and has a fine coat and thick, silky mane and tail hair. It stands between 16 and 17hh (163–173cm).

Boulonnais

The Boulonnais comes from the area round Boulogne, in northeast France. Two types of Boulonnais were bred – one was a heavy farm worker and the other was a lighter, faster horse called a *mareyeur* (meaning 'fish-seller'). This horse was used for transporting fish from the coast to Paris.

Fast action

The Boulonnais can move faster than most heavy horses and has lower knee action. Some still work on farms, but to ensure the breed does not die out, the French government breeds Boulonnais.

Percheron

This powerful breed comes from La Perche in northern France. Its ancestors carried knights who wore heavy armour. In the 18th century, the Percheron was crossed with Arabs, giving it greater quality and better action. The horses are clean-legged, a great advantage when they worked on the land.

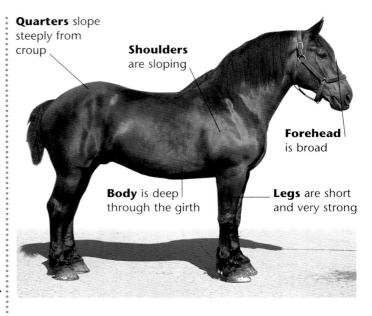

Quarters slope steeply from croup

Shoulders are sloping

Forehead is broad

Body is deep through the girth

Legs are short and very strong

Facts and figures

- **Place of origin**
  Normandy, France

- **Height**
  16.1–17.2hh (165–178cm)

- **Colour**
  Grey or black

- **Uses**
  Farm work; coaching

One of the tallest horses that has ever lived was a Percheron. It stood 21hh (213cm), though not many of them are as large as that. Percherons are broad, compact and very strong with sturdy legs and good feet. The breed has a more elegant appearance, lower action and a finer head than most heavy breeds because of its Arab blood.

Carriage horses
Although some Percherons still work on the land, they are also popular as carriage horses. Despite being so large, they have a low, free action and move easily. They are docile and work well.

Suffolk

Often called the Suffolk Punch, this is the most pure-bred of all Britain's heavy horses. All Suffolks are descended from one stallion called the Horse of Ufford, which was born in 1768. The Suffolk is stocky with short legs, and is always chestnut in colour. Some Suffolks are used for farm work, but the breed is now mostly seen in the show ring.

Suffolk foal
Suffolks mature early and live for a long time. This foal may start its working life at two years old, and continue for many years. Suffolks are valuable as both farm horses and draught horses in towns.

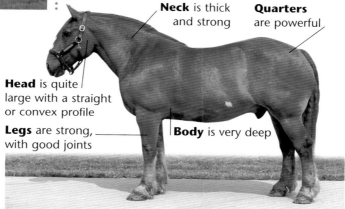

Neck is thick and strong

Quarters are powerful

Head is quite large with a straight or convex profile

Legs are strong, with good joints

Body is very deep

The Suffolk has a round, barrel-shaped body on short, strong legs. Its chest is wide, and it has a thick neck with low withers. Despite its bulk, the horse moves freely and has an energetic trot. It has a friendly and docile temperament, and is easy to handle.

Key facts

- **Place of origin**
  Suffolk, England

- **Height**
  16–16.3hh
  (163–170cm)

- **Colour**
  Always chestnut, with no white markings except on the face

Farm horse

The Suffolk was bred to work on farms in eastern England. The lack of feather on its legs is an advantage, as it means that the heavy clay soil does not cling to them. Suffolks do not need a lot of food, which makes them cheap to keep.

Shire

Tall and extremely strong, the Shire is probably the heaviest of England's heavy horses. It can weigh up to 1,219kg and may stand up to 17.2hh (178cm). Some are even taller. Its girth can measure up to 2.4m. The Shire gets its name from the English counties where it was bred (Derbyshire, Staffordshire, Lincolnshire and Leicestershire). Shire horses often worked on farms. Many brewers also used them to pull carts called drays to deliver beer in cities.

Knights' horse

In medieval times, the Shire was called 'the great horse of England'. Its size and strength made it the ideal horse for carrying knights in armour, who could weigh up to 190kg. This breed was also an all-round workhorse, employed on farms and wherever great pulling power was needed.

Ploughing match

There are not many working Shire horses today, but they are often seen at ploughing matches and shows. Their manes are braided and plumed, and their bridles and harness gleam with polished brasses. They are a magnificent sight, and their strength and gentleness are much admired.

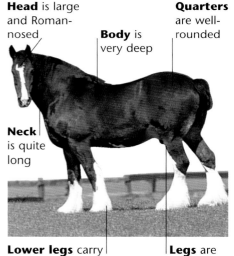

Head is large and Roman-nosed

Body is very deep

Quarters are well-rounded

Neck is quite long

Lower legs carry lots of feather

Legs are very strong

This tall and extremely powerful horse is able to pull five times its own weight. A Shire is usually black, bay, brown or grey in colour. Its legs often have long white stockings, and the feather is fine and silky. Shires' tails are often cut short, which means that they lose their natural fly whisks.

Kindly horse

The Shire has a broad forehead. The large eyes have a kindly expression, which shows how gentle this breed can be. The face often has a broad white blaze that goes over the nose and the muzzle.

Neck is thick and arched

Facts and figures

- **Place of origin**
  English Midlands

- **Height**
  16.2–17.2hh (168–178cm)

- **Colour**
  Bay, brown, black or grey

- **Uses**
  As dray horses; for showing

Clydesdale

The Clydesdale is related to the Shire, but is lighter in build. This breed comes from Scotland, where it was originally used for farm work. Later it was used to pull various forms of transport, including coal wagons. Today, the Clydesdale is seen at shows and in ploughing matches. It is also crossed with Thoroughbreds to produce heavyweight riding horses.

Clydesdales are usually bay, brown, black or roan. They often have white markings that start at their feet and go right up the legs. Some cover part of the horse's belly, and the face may be mostly white, too. These big horses stand about 16.2 to 17hh (168–173cm).

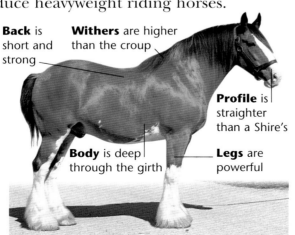

Back is short and strong

Withers are higher than the croup

Profile is straighter than a Shire's

Body is deep through the girth

Legs are powerful

Trade turnout

Beautifully decorated Clydesdales are often seen at shows, harnessed to brightly painted vehicles called trade turnouts.

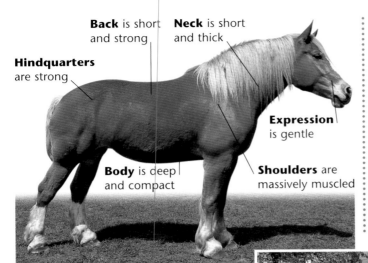

Back is short and strong

Neck is short and thick

Hindquarters are strong

Expression is gentle

Body is deep and compact

Shoulders are massively muscled

Brabant

This ancient breed dates back to Roman times and is also known as the Brabançon and Belgian Heavy Draught. The Brabant's ancestors were warhorses, and they helped create the Shire, Clydesdale and possibly the Suffolk. The breeding of Brabants was carefully controlled to produce an impressive horse.

Standing 16 to 17hh (163 to 173cm), the Brabant is a compact, very strong horse. It is usually chestnut or red roan in colour. This breed of horse is good-natured and intelligent. It is a popular breed in the United States, as well as in its native Belgium.

Still working

The Brabant is not used much for farm work nowadays, but can still be seen working in harness. This pair is pulling a bus through the streets of a small, European-style town in California.

Noriker

This Austrian breed dates back to the 16th century. Its name comes from the word 'Noricum', which was a Roman province situated where Austria is now. The Noriker is related to the Haflinger, and was bred to work on the farms and forests of the Austrian Alps. It is strong, hard-working and easy to handle.

Mane and **tail** are often flaxen

Back is long

Nostrils are wide

Legs are strong and carry little feather

Girth is massive

Broad horse

The Noriker has a broad chest, and its girth measurement should not be less than 60 per cent of its height. It has short, sturdy legs. This breed's tough constitution helps it to withstand the harsh Alpine winters.

The Noriker stands between 16 and 17hh (163–173cm) and is chestnut, brown or black in colour. The legs are strong, and its action is longer and lower than that of many heavy breeds. It has a calm temperament, is sure-footed and economical to keep.

Friesian

This attractive breed from the Netherlands was the mount of German and Friesian knights during the Crusades. It was used for farm work, and in the 19th century, for trotting races. Friesians are still ridden sometimes, but they are used mostly as carriage horses. As they are black, they are often used for funerals.

Neck is arched and carried high

Quarters slope from croup

Expression is alert

Legs are quite long and well-feathered

Body is not very deep

Four-in-hand

Friesians are popular driving horses. They look very smart and they have a fast, high-stepping trot. This team, called a four-in-hand, is owned by Harrods, London's famous department store.

Standing between 15 and 16hh (152–163cm), the Friesian is black all over, though some may have a small white star on their foreheads. The horse is lighter in build than many heavy breeds. The Friesian has a good temperament and is easy to handle.

Neck is short and huge

Quarters slope steeply from the croup

Dutch Draught

This breed is believed to be the most massively built of all European heavy draught horses. It was developed in the late 19th and early 20th centuries from Ardennais and native horses. The Royal Dutch Draught Horse Society controls its breeding. The result is a very heavy and powerful working horse.

Head has a straight profile

Legs carry a lot of feather

Shoulders are muscular

Legs have huge muscles

The Dutch Draught stands about 16.3hh (170cm) and is usually chestnut, bay, roan, grey or black in colour. Although it is very heavy, its action is free and active. This breed matures early and is long-lived. The Dutch Draught has a quiet nature and is a good worker.

Show horse

Today, Dutch Draughts are mostly seen in the show ring, where they may be driven to a variety of carts. Some, however, are still used to pull vehicles around city streets, selling or advertizing goods.

Warmblood horses

Most of the horse and pony breeds throughout the world are classed as 'warmbloods'. Many types of horses and ponies also belong to this group. Warmblood horses include the highly successful German and Dutch competition horses, and most of the American breeds.

Swedish Warmblood

Bred from Spanish, oriental and Friesian horses in the 17th century, the Swedish Warmblood was a cavalry horse. Later, the breed was crossed with Thoroughbreds, Trakehners, Hanoverians and Arabs. Today, it is a competition horse, good at jumping, eventing and dressage.

Standing around 16.2 to 17hh (168–173cm), the Swedish Warmblood is a big, athletic horse. It has powerful shoulders and quarters, strong legs and good feet. Its calm temperament and sensible attitude help make it good at dressage. It can be any solid colour.

Hindquarters are powerful

Neck is long

Head is elegant

Shoulders are deep and powerful

Body is deep through the girth

Selle Français

The Selle Français (meaning 'French saddle') was bred in Normandy, France, in the 19th century, from native Norman horses and imported English Thoroughbreds. In the middle of the 20th century, French Trotters, Thoroughbreds, Arabs and Anglo-Arabs were used to develop the breed.

The Selle Français is a well-built horse, with strong legs and lots of muscle. Its body is quite long, and its withers are high. It stands about 16hh (163cm). It is intelligent, with a calm temperament, and is agile and athletic. It may be any solid colour.

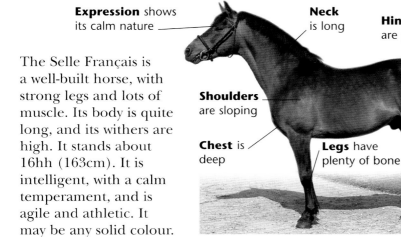

Expression shows its calm nature

Neck is long

Hindquarters are powerful

Shoulders are sloping

Chest is deep

Legs have plenty of bone

Good jumper

This horse excels at showjumping and eventing. It tackles difficult cross-country fences bravely, and is good at dressage. It makes a good all-round riding horse. In France, some Selle Français are bred especially for racing.

Competition breeds

Although many breeds and types of horse are good at dressage, eventing and showjumping, the breeds described here are particularly well known for it. They were produced by crossing farm and carriage horses with English Thoroughbreds. This made lighter, faster horses, which kept the calmer nature of the heavier animals.

Quarters are muscular and powerful

Neck is long

Shoulders are sloping

Legs are strong, with plenty of bone

Body is deep through the girth

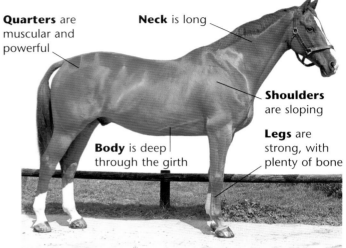

Dutch Warmblood

This breed was created in the 20th century by crossing the Gelderlander and the Groningen with the English Thoroughbred. It is possibly the most successful of the competition breeds. These horses are strong and athletic, with a calm temperament.

Quarters are well-muscled

Body is deep through the girth

Withers are high

Head may be plain

Legs are strong

Shoulders are powerful

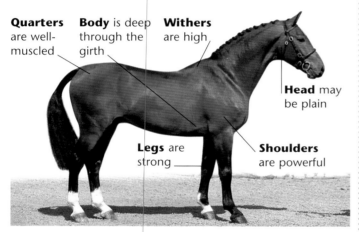

Hanoverian

This breed was developed in the 18th century by crossing Holsteins with local mares. This produced a strong horse that was used for farm work. Trakehners and English Thoroughbreds were used to improve the breed and create a first-class competition horse.

Dressage champion
Strong, athletic and with good action, this breed is superb at dressage. This picture shows Isabell Werth on Nissan Gigolo riding for Germany.

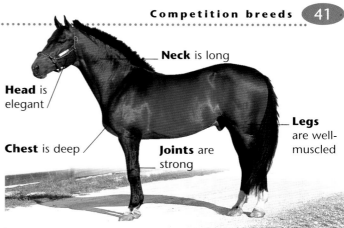

Head is elegant

Neck is long

Chest is deep

Joints are strong

Legs are well-muscled

Famous partnership
One of the most famous dressage partnerships of all time was Jennie Loriston-Clarke and Dutch Courage, here giving a demonstration of long-reining.

Holstein

Between the 17th and 19th centuries, Holsteins were used as carriage horses. Since the 19th century, they have been bred for riding. They are excellent at cross-country, and do well in dressage and showjumping.

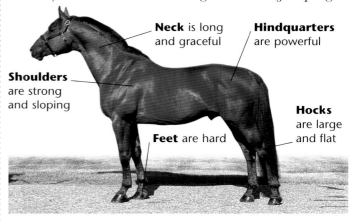

Neck is long and graceful

Hindquarters are powerful

Shoulders are strong and sloping

Hocks are large and flat

Feet are hard

Trakehner

This breed began in East Prussia in the 13th century. Originally a carriage horse, it was crossed with Arabs and Thoroughbreds to produce cavalry horses. It is a first-class dressage, jumping and eventing competitor.

Marius, the highly successful Dutch Warmblood stallion, jumping in Calgary, Canada, in 1979.

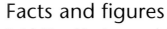

Facts and figures

Dutch Warmblood
- **Height**
  15.3–16.3hh (160–170cm)

- **Colour**
  Any solid colour

Hanoverian
- **Height**
  16–17hh (163–173cm)

- **Colour**
  Any solid colour

Holstein
- **Height**
  16–17hh (163–173cm)

- **Colour**
  Any solid colour

Trakehner
- **Height**
  16–17.2hh (163–178cm)

- **Colour**
  Any solid colour

Oldenburg

The tallest and heaviest of the German warmblood breeds, the Oldenburg was bred in the 17th century as a coach horse. It was named after the area of Germany from which it came, and the man who bred it, Count Anton von Oldenburg. Its ancestors include Friesian, Neapolitan, Spanish, Cleveland Bay, English Thoroughbred and Norfolk Roadster horses. Today, it is used for driving, dressage and showjumping.

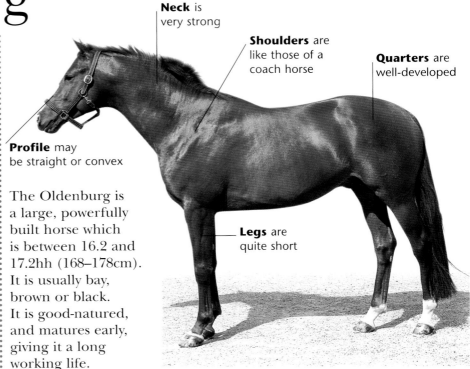

Neck is very strong

Shoulders are like those of a coach horse

Quarters are well-developed

Profile may be straight or convex

Legs are quite short

The Oldenburg is a large, powerfully built horse which is between 16.2 and 17.2hh (168–178cm). It is usually bay, brown or black. It is good-natured, and matures early, giving it a long working life.

Gelderlander

This breed comes from the Gelder area of the Netherlands, where it has been bred since the 19th century. Gelderlanders were then used mainly as carriage horses, but they were also expected to do light farm work and double as riding horses. Their ancestors include the Oldenburg and the Thoroughbred.

The heavily built Gelderlander stands 15.2 to 16.2hh (157–168cm), and is usually chestnut in colour. It often has a wide white blaze on its face and white stockings on its legs. Although it is not thought of as a beautiful horse, it is very strong. The Gelderlander has a gentle, docile temperament, making it easy to handle.

Tail is set high

Shoulders are upright

Head is large and plain

Legs are strong

Carriage horses

Although Gelderlanders are no longer used for farm work, they are still popular carriage horses, and are used in driving competitions. They are also useful heavyweight riding horses, due to their size and strong build. These horses are not fast, but they are good jumpers.

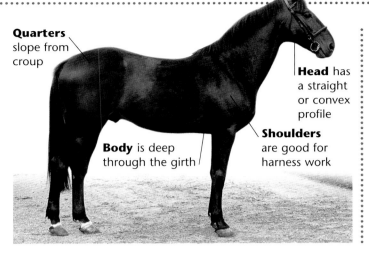

Quarters slope from croup

Head has a straight or convex profile

Body is deep through the girth

Shoulders are good for harness work

French Trotter

This breed was developed in Normandy, France, in the 19th century, to compete in the new sport of trotting. The first trotting racecourse in France was opened in Cherbourg in 1836. The French Trotter's ancestors were the Norfolk Trotter, the English Thoroughbred and horses from the Normandy region.

The French Trotter is about 16.2hh (168cm). It may be any solid colour, but is usually bay, brown or chestnut. Strong and tough, with long legs, these horses have free-striding, active action, great stamina and are willing workers.

Racing sulkies

French Trotters are generally raced in harness. The light, two-wheeled vehicles they pull are called sulkies. They are also raced under saddle. Some French Trotters are used for general riding and for breeding riding horses. They are good jumpers.

Camargue

The Camargue region of the Rhône delta in France is a bleak and windy area. Here, the wild Camargue horses have lived on poor grazing for thousands of years. Some are tamed and ridden by local cowboys to round up wild black bulls.

Wild white horses

Camargue ponies have been called the 'wild white horses of the sea'. They are small at 14hh (142cm), very tough and always white or grey in colour. They look like the horses in ancient cave paintings.

Przewalski's Horse

In the late 1870s, a Russian explorer named Nicolai Przewalski discovered a herd of pony-sized wild horses in the mountains of Mongolia, on the edge of the Gobi Desert. They looked similar to the primitive herds that once roamed Asia, and became known as Przewalski's Horse. Also called the Mongolian or Asiatic Wild Horse, Przewalski's Horse and the Tarpan are two surviving strains of four types of primitive horses which existed 10,000 years ago.

The breed saved
Przewalski's Horse is now extinct in the wild, but it is preserved in zoos and private studs.

Stone Age horse

Between 16,000 and 27,000 years ago, early humans painted animals on the walls of caves. Some of the pictures were of horses that looked like the animal we call Przewalski's Horse. Amazingly, this breed has hardly changed at all over this long period of time.

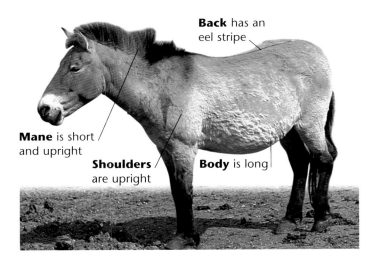

Back has an eel stripe

Mane is short and upright

Shoulders are upright

Body is long

Facts and figures

Przewalski's Horse
- **Height**
  12–14.2hh (122–147cm)
- **Colour**
  Yellow dun, with black points

Tarpan
- **Height**
  Around 13hh (132cm)
- **Colour**
  Mouse dun, brown

Przewalski's Horse has similar features to primitive horses. The body is dun with black points, and the legs may have zebra stripes. On the back is a black line called an eel stripe. The mane grows upright and there is little or no forelock. The muzzle and the areas around the eyes are pale in colour.

Face to face
Przewalski's Horses have large, plain heads with a convex or straight profile. Their eyes are set high up, so their heads look long.

Tarpan

The Tarpan originally lived in Russia and in central and eastern Europe. The breed was domesticated, but in the 19th century, it became extinct. In the 1930s, a Polish professor named Vetulani found ponies living in Polish forests that were like the ancient breed. With careful breeding, he recreated the Tarpan.

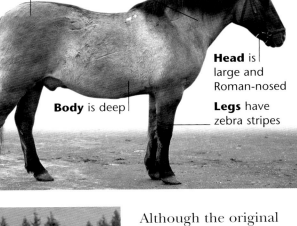

Quarters slope steeply

Neck is short and thick

Head is large and Roman-nosed

Body is deep

Legs have zebra stripes

Modern Tarpan

The new breed of Tarpan lives a natural life in herds on reserves owned by the Polish government. Despite its ancient ancestry, it is much less primitive-looking than Przewalski's Horse. Although its head is quite big and its neck is quite short, the Tarpan looks much more like a modern riding pony.

Although the original Tarpan is extinct, Professor Vetulani's new breed is so similar to the old one that some people consider it still exists. Like Przewalski's Horse, it has a dorsal stripe and zebra stripes on the legs. The Tarpan's mane and tail are long.

Irish Draught

The Irish Draught was bred in its native Ireland as an all-round horse used for riding, driving and farm work. This breed dates back to the 12th century, and its ancestors include European heavy breeds and the Spanish Horse. It is large and strong, and capable of carrying a lot of weight.

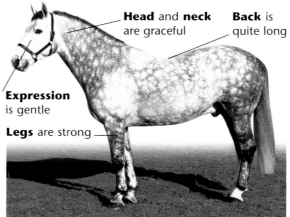

Head and **neck** are graceful

Back is quite long

Expression is gentle

Legs are strong

Natural jumper

This breed is a natural jumper. Both the pure-bred Irish Draught and the Thoroughbred cross are often used for hunting. They can clear all kinds of obstacles when ridden on cross-country courses.

Despite its size – 16 to 17hh (163–173cm) – the Irish Draught is economical to keep. It has a calm temperament, and is easy to ride and handle. It can be any solid colour, but is often grey. Although it is not very fast, this big horse is athletic and agile.

Hackney Horse

The Hackney Horse is an English breed that developed from two earlier breeds called the Norfolk Trotter and the Yorkshire Roadster. These were heavier, working horses, but the modern Hackney is more graceful because it was cross-bred with Thoroughbreds. The Hackney is now a show harness horse that delights spectators with its brilliant action and appearance.

This lightly built and compact horse gives the impression of having great energy. It is high-spirited and moves very freely, throwing its forelegs well forwards with each stride. The action must be straight when seen from the front or the back.

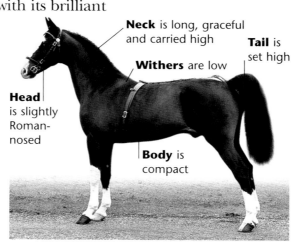

Neck is long, graceful and carried high

Tail is set high

Withers are low

Head is slightly Roman-nosed

Body is compact

High-stepping horse

The Hackney's action, especially when trotting, is spectacular. It raises its knees and hocks very high, and as it moves, pauses slightly at each stride, giving the impression of an effortless, floating movement.

Cleveland Bay

This is the oldest of the native British breeds. It has been bred in the north of England since the Middle Ages. Apart from Barb and Spanish crosses in the 17th century, the breed has been kept pure. These horses are strong, hardy, long-lived and good-natured.

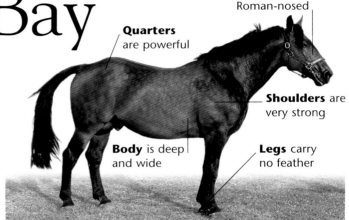

Head is large and Roman-nosed

Quarters are powerful

Shoulders are very strong

Body is deep and wide

Legs carry no feather

The Cleveland Bay is now classed as a rare breed. It is not used as a carriage horse so much nowadays, and is mainly used to cross with other breeds. As a result, the pure-bred Cleveland has almost disappeared.

Royal team

The Royal Mews at Buckingham Palace in London, England, has Cleveland Bays, which pull the royal carriages. The Duke of Edinburgh (left) is driving a four-in-hand team, which competes in cross-country driving events.

Key facts

- **Place of origin**
  North Yorkshire, England

- **Height**
  About 16.2hh (168cm)

- **Colour**
  Always bay with no white except a star

- **Uses**
  Driving, sometimes riding

Andalucian

The Andalucian horse, from southern Spain, is the modern equivalent of the ancient Spanish Horse, which influenced horse breeding worldwide. Most American breeds are descended from the Spanish Horse. The Andalucian is noble and proud, agile and athletic, with a good temperament.

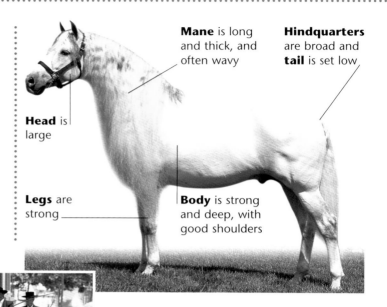

Mane is long and thick, and often wavy

Hindquarters are broad and **tail** is set low

Head is large

Legs are strong

Body is strong and deep, with good shoulders

Ride and drive

Although it is mainly used for riding, and is a popular dressage horse, the Andalucian is also driven. In its native Spain, it is often used in harness during ceremonial and festive occasions.

The beautiful Andalucian horse stands between 15 and 16hh (152–163cm). It is bay or grey in colour, the grey sometimes having a pinkish tone. The Andalucian carries itself proudly, is athletic, although not fast, and has a kind and friendly nature.

Lusitano

The Lusitano is similar to the Andalucian breed and is also descended from the Spanish Horse. It comes from Portugal, and was used by the Portuguese cavalry and for light farm work. This horse has spectacular high action, and it is taught 'high school' movements. It is also used as a carriage horse.

Mane and **tail** are full, long and often wavy

Hindquarters are sloping and **hindlegs** are long

Profile is straight or Roman-nosed

Cannon bones are long

Back is short, and ribs are well rounded

Spanish walk

This horse is performing a special 'high school' movement called the Spanish walk, which it has been trained to do. In this gait, the forelegs are lifted up high and stretched out in front of the horse.

The Lusitano stands between 15 and 16hh (152–163cm), and it can be any solid colour. Grey is the most common colour, but this horse may also be bay, dun, chestnut or black. The Lusitano has a short, arched neck, sloping quarters and a compact body.

Lipizzaner

The Lipizzaner is the horse used by the famous Spanish Riding School of Vienna, in Austria. It is descended from the ancient Spanish breed, which is how the school got its name. The word 'Lipizzaner' comes from Lipica, in Slovenia, where these horses were originally bred.

Stocky horse

The Lipizzaner is stockily built, with short, strong legs. The shape of this horse's shoulders makes it suitable for use in harness as well as for riding. Its action tends to be high, and its feet are strong. It is an extremely intelligent horse.

Spanish school

The Spanish Riding School trains Lipizzaner stallions to perform high school movements in an 18th-century arena lit by large chandeliers. It takes many years to train both the horses and their riders.

From black to grey
Lipizzaner foals are born black, and their coats gradually get lighter in colour as they grow older. They may be seven years or even older before they turn grey.

Key facts
- **Place of origin**
  Lipica, Slovenia
- **Height**
  15.1–16.2hh
  (155–168cm)
- **Colour**
  Usually grey, but sometimes bay
- **Uses**
  General riding, and as a carriage horse
- **Characteristics**
  Intelligent, docile and long-lived

Head is often Roman-nosed

Hindquarters are powerful

Body is long and **withers** low

Neck is short and thick

Levade
The 'levade' is a classical high school movement. The horse rears up and balances on its hind legs.

Legs are powerful

Morgan

The Morgan comes from the eastern states of Massachusetts and Vermont in the USA. Morgans are descended from a stallion born in 1789, named Justin Morgan, after his owner. This horse worked on the farm, and raced, both in harness and under saddle.

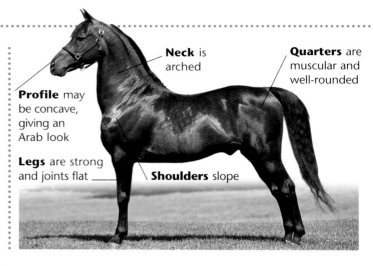

Profile may be concave, giving an Arab look

Neck is arched

Quarters are muscular and well-rounded

Legs are strong and joints flat

Shoulders slope

Specially shod

Morgans are shown in either Park or Pleasure classes. Horses shown in the Park classes have their feet trimmed and shod to produce a high action. If this is not done, the action is normal.

Standing between 14.2 and 15.2hh (147–157cm), the Morgan is bay, brown, chestnut or black in colour. It is spirited, intelligent and alert, but has a good temperament, and is easy to handle. Hardy, strong and full of stamina, it is both ridden and driven.

Criollo

Descended from Spanish horses brought to South America in the 16th century, the Criollo is considered to be the toughest and soundest breed of horse in the world. The breed is native to the grassy plains of Argentina, where it is used by the gauchos, or cowboys, to work cattle. The Criollo is also found in Brazil, Uruguay, Chile, Peru and Venezuela.

The Criollo can survive on little food in harsh climates. It is long-lived, and has great stamina. In the 1920s, Professor Aimé Tschiffely rode two Criollo ponies, called Mancha and Gato, from Buenos Aires in South America to New York in the USA. The total distance was 16,000km.

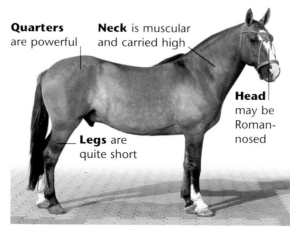

Quarters are powerful

Neck is muscular and carried high

Head may be Roman-nosed

Legs are quite short

Polo pony

Criollos are 14 to 15hh (142–152cm) and are usually dun in colour, with dark points and an eel stripe. They are often crossed with Thoroughbreds to produce the famous Argentinian polo ponies.

Quarter Horse

This first 'all-American' horse was bred in Virginia in the 17th century for riding and farm work. Its speed and agility made it perfect for working cattle. The breed is so-named because English settlers used to race these horses over quarter-mile (402m) tracks.

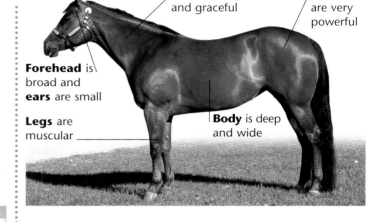

Neck is long and graceful

Quarters are very powerful

Forehead is broad and **ears** are small

Legs are muscular

Body is deep and wide

Facts and figures

- **Place of origin**
  Virginia, USA
- **Height**
  15–16hh (152–163cm)
- **Colour**
  Any solid colour
- **Uses**
  Working cattle, showing

It has been claimed that the Quarter Horse is the most popular horse in the world, with over three million registered in the USA. Agile and athletic, yet with a calm temperament, it is an ideal riding horse, as well as being superb at working cattle and performing at Western horse shows.

Sliding halt

A horse that works with cattle must be able to start, stop and turn very quickly. In Western horse shows, one of the most dramatic movements is the sliding halt, where the horse stops instantly (right). Special shoes on the hind feet allow them to slide.

Pinto

The Pinto is a colour type rather than a breed, though there are two Pinto breed societies in the United States. Descended from 16th-century Spanish horses, it has become popular in the United States. Pintos can be black and white (piebald), or chestnut or brown and white (skewbald).

'Pinto' comes from the Spanish word *pintado*, which means 'painted'. There are two main colour types: overo, which is mostly coloured with white patches, and tobiano, which is mostly white with coloured patches (rearing horse, far right). Pintos may vary in size and shape.

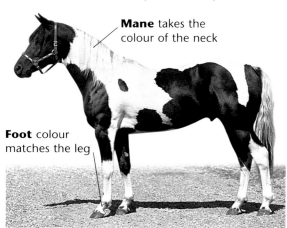

Mane takes the colour of the neck

Foot colour matches the leg

Native favourites

Pintos were favourites of the Native Americans because their colouring provided good camouflage. Today, they are often bred for their colour rather than their shape, and points are awarded for their markings.

Palomino

This is another colour type rather than a breed, so Palominos may be any size. The coat colour should be as near as possible to that of a new gold coin, with a white mane and tail. Palominos were brought to the USA by the Spanish in the 15th and 16th centuries.

Mane and **tail** are white

Coat is golden

White socks must not go above the hocks

Head may have small white markings

Barrel racing

Palominos are bred by crossing palomino-coloured horses with chestnuts, or chestnuts with creams or albinos. In 15th-century Spain, the palomino colour was a favourite of the powerful Queen Isabella.

Palominos may be of any size or type and can be used for many activities, including showing and Western classes, as well as for general riding. This horse is negotiating a tight turn at a gallop as part of a barrel race in Tampa, Florida.

Appaloosa

This breed gets its name from the Palouse River in Washington State, USA. It was bred as a workhorse by the Nez Percé tribe of native Americans in the 18th century, from imported Spanish horses. Quarter Horses have been used to improve the breed, making it a strong, compact and good-natured horse. It is agile and athletic, has great stamina and is a good jumper.

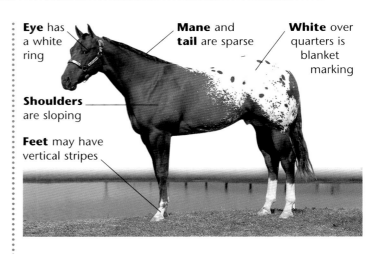

Eye has a white ring

Mane and **tail** are sparse

White over quarters is blanket marking

Shoulders are sloping

Feet may have vertical stripes

The main markings are leopard (white coat with dark spots – below); frost (dark background with white speckles); blanket (white quarters and loins, sometimes with dark spots); marble (roan, with a frost pattern in the centre of the body and darker round the edges); and snowflake (dark background with white spots).

Facts and figures

- **Place of origin**
  Washington State, USA

- **Height**
  14.2–15.2hh (147–157cm)

- **Colour**
  White with dark markings

- **Uses**
  Riding, showing, jumping

Tennessee Walking Horse

This breed was developed in the 18th and 19th centuries by plantation, or estate, owners of the southern United States, who wanted a comfortable riding horse to carry them round their large areas of land. It is called a 'gaited horse', because it can perform three extra gaits – the flat walk, the running walk and the rocking-chair canter. All these movements are smooth and comfortable for the rider.

The Tennessee Walking Horse is a popular riding horse for all members of the family in the USA, as well as a show horse. The breed stands 15 to 16hh (152–163cm) and is usually brown, bay, chestnut or black. It is said to be the most good-tempered of all horses.

Mane is clipped off at the top in the USA

Head is large

Shoulders are muscular

Tail is set high

Back is short

Legs are strong

American Saddlebred

The Saddlebred was bred in Kentucky, USA, in the 19th century. It is another 'gaited' horse: three-gaited horses perform the walk, trot and canter with high steps; five-gaited horses also perform the slow gait and the rack, both four-beat, lateral paces. The way the horse is shod accentuates its action.

The Saddlebred is usually bay, brown or chestnut, and stands 15 to 16hh (152–163cm). Nicking the dock muscles makes it carry its tail higher. It is mostly a show horse, but if it is shod normally, it can be used for harness or general riding.

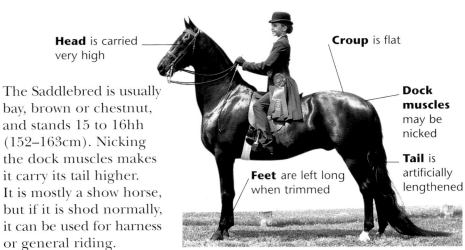

Head is carried very high

Croup is flat

Dock muscles may be nicked

Tail is artificially lengthened

Feet are left long when trimmed

Spectacular action

The rack (above) is a fast and spectacular pace in which each leg is raised high and lands separately. Special boots protect the front heels and pasterns from being injured by the horse's hind feet as they reach far forwards.

Missouri Foxtrotter

This horse was bred in the 19th century in Arkansas and Missouri in the USA as a comfortable riding horse that could cover long distances quite quickly. The breed has a unique gait called a 'foxtrot', in which it walks with its front legs and trots with its hind legs.

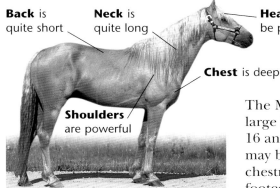

Back is quite short

Neck is quite long

Head may be plain

Chest is deep

Shoulders are powerful

The Missouri Foxtrotter is a large horse which stands between 16 and 17hh (163–173 cm). It may be any colour, but most are chestnut. This breed is sure-footed and has a gentle nature.

Comfortable ride

The Foxtrotter's gait is smooth and comfortable. It can travel at a speed of 8km/h for long distances, and may go twice as fast over shorter distances. This breed is used for trail riding and showing.

Standardbred

The Standardbred is the fastest harness racing horse in the world. It was first bred in the USA in the 19th century. Most Standardbreds are descended from an English Thoroughbred, which also had Norfolk Trotter ancestors. Standardbreds race either as trotters or pacers.

The Standardbred is about 15.2hh (157cm) and is usually bay, brown or chestnut. More heavily built than the Thoroughbred, it is fast and has great stamina. This horse can cover 1.6km in one minute 54 seconds.

Head and **neck** are carried high

Croup is higher than withers

Hindquarters are very powerful

Head is quite plain

Chest is deep

Legs are strong and sturdy

Mustang

The tough wild horses that once roamed the plains of the western USA are called Mustangs. They are descended from Spanish horses taken to America in the 16th century, which were turned loose or escaped and became wild. For centuries, Mustangs lived a natural life. Today, special efforts are made to protect the original type of wild horse.

Mustangs range in height from 13.2 to 15hh (137–152cm) and may be any colour. They are fast, strong, agile and hardy. They do not always have good natures, but some are domesticated and used as riding and endurance horses.

Head may be Roman-nosed

Legs are strong and tough

Body is compact

In the wild

Mustangs were rounded up and used by cowboys for cattle herding. Some were tamed and ridden by Native Americans, and others were hunted. As a result, their numbers fell, but they are now protected by US law.

Waler

The oddly named Waler is Australian – its name comes from 'New South Wales'. It was bred from Basuto ponies, Arabs, Barbs and Thoroughbreds to work on the huge Australian cattle and sheep ranches. It was a cavalry horse in the Boer War and the First World War. It is also now used for police work.

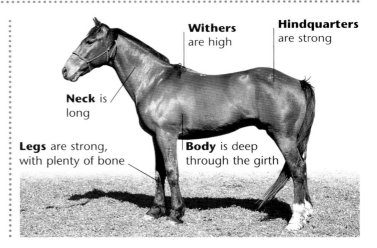

Withers are high

Hindquarters are strong

Neck is long

Legs are strong, with plenty of bone

Body is deep through the girth

Riding horse

The Waler is sometimes called the Australian Stock Horse, but it is also an ideal horse for general riding. It is fast and agile and is a natural jumper. Some Walers perform at rodeos, doing displays of buckjumping.

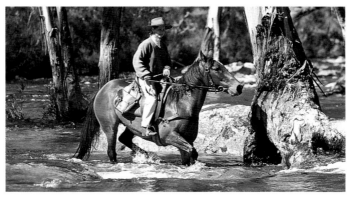

The Waler ranges in height from 14.2 to 16hh (147–163cm) and may be any solid colour. It is more powerfully built than the Thoroughbred. It is strong and tough, and its great powers of endurance mean that it can be ridden round the ranch all day.

Pony
breeds

Ponies are smaller than horses and have different features. They are deeper through the girth and have shorter legs. They often have feather on the lower legs, and thick manes and tails. Ponies are sure-footed, and usually full of character.

Dartmoor

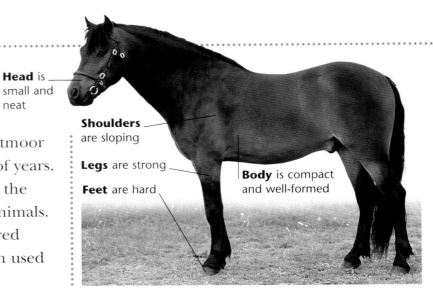

Head is small and neat

Shoulders are sloping

Legs are strong

Feet are hard

Body is compact and well-formed

Small ponies have lived wild on Dartmoor in Devon, England, for hundreds of years. Poor grazing and harsh conditions on the moors have produced strong, tough animals. Over the centuries, Arab, Thoroughbred and Welsh Section A crosses have been used to improve the quality of this breed.

The Dartmoor is a first-class children's riding pony. It is strong enough to carry a heavy weight, has good paces, jumps well and has a good temperament. It stands around 12.2hh (127cm) and is bay or brown in colour.

Wild on the moor

There are not many pure-bred ponies living wild on Dartmoor today. Most of them are bred in studs. The ponies roaming the moor look quite different. In winter, to withstand the wind, rain and snow of their native home, they grow very thick coats and long, shaggy manes and tails.

Exmoor

This pony is from the region of southwest England known as Exmoor. It is one of the oldest breeds in the world, and dates back to the Ice Age. Today it is classed as a rare breed. It is only 12.2 to 12.3hh (127–130cm), but is strong enough to carry an adult.

Eye is hooded, with a light ring round it, called a 'toad' eye

Muzzle is light-coloured

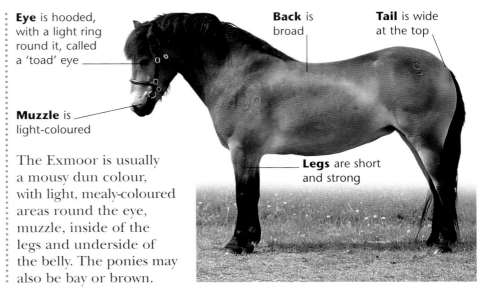

Back is broad

Tail is wide at the top

Legs are short and strong

The Exmoor is usually a mousy dun colour, with light, mealy-coloured areas round the eye, muzzle, inside of the legs and underside of the belly. The ponies may also be bay or brown.

Head is small and neat

Hindquarters are strong and give speed and jumping ability

Shoulders are sloping

Legs are strong, with plenty of bone

Body is compact and deep through the girth

Connemara

The Connemara comes from the moors of western Ireland, where its ancestors have lived since the 16th century. Native ponies were crossed with Spanish, Barb, Arab, Welsh Cob and Thoroughbred horses to develop the breed. The result is a strong, sturdy riding pony, with good paces and jumping ability.

Connemaras can be grey, dun, bay, brown, black, chestnut or roan. They are 13 to 14.2hh (132–147cm) and are hardy, docile and intelligent. They are ridden by both children and adults, and make good competition horses when crossed with Thoroughbreds.

New Forest

Since the 11th century, ponies have lived in the New Forest in Hampshire, England. Over the years, different breeds have been introduced, as well as Arabs and Barbs, so New Forest ponies have a mixture of ancestors. They are fast and have good, low action.

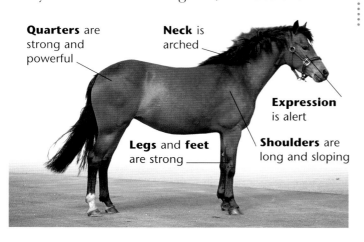

Quarters are strong and powerful

Neck is arched

Expression is alert

Legs and **feet** are strong

Shoulders are long and sloping

Forest pony

There are two types of pony – one stands up to 13.1hh (135cm), and the other 13.2 to 14.2hh (137–147cm). Both are narrow in build, making them easy for children to ride. The ponies may be of any solid colour.

Most of the New Forest is heathland. Local people, known as Commoners, are allowed to keep ponies there. Many of these are in poor condition. The better examples of the breed usually come from stud farms.

Welsh Section A

The Welsh Section A, or Welsh Mountain Pony, has lived on the hills of Wales in Britain since pre-Roman times. It is thought to be the most beautiful pony breed. Strong and tough, with great powers of endurance, it is used for riding and driving.

Section A ponies should not be taller than 12hh (122cm). They look like miniature Arabs, and are strong for their size. They may be any solid colour, are sure-footed and intelligent, and make good riding ponies.

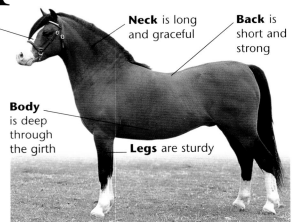

Head is small and dished

Neck is long and graceful

Back is short and strong

Body is deep through the girth

Legs are sturdy

Welsh Section B

The Welsh Section B is also called the Welsh Pony. It was bred by crossing Section As with Section Ds, and has Arab ancestors as well. Originally the pony was used by farmers for transport and for herding sheep grazing on the Welsh hills. The modern type of this breed has existed since the early 20th century.

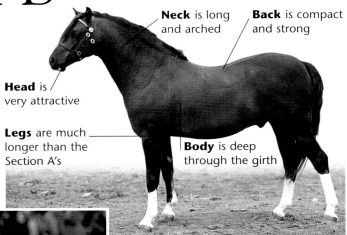

Neck is long and arched

Back is compact and strong

Head is very attractive

Legs are much longer than the Section A's

Body is deep through the girth

Section B ponies are 12.2 to 13.2hh (127–137cm) and may be any solid colour. They have the character and gentle nature of the Section A, but make more useful riding ponies because of their longer legs.

Competitive pony

As the Section B is taller than the Welsh Mountain Pony, it can be ridden by larger children and used in competitions such as gymkhana events. It has long, low action, and is also a good jumper.

Welsh Section C

This pony was originally bred by crossing the Section A and Section D, and is known as the Welsh Pony of Cob Type. Smaller than the Welsh Cob, but stockier in build than the Welsh Pony, it was once used for all kinds of farm work, as well as in the slate quarries of North Wales. Today it is often used for trekking and trail riding, as well as driving.

Neck is thick and carried high

Quarters are very muscular

Head is attractive

Shoulders are powerful

Legs are strong

This small pony should not be taller than 13.2hh (137cm). Despite its size, the Section C is very strong. It is also hardy enough to live outside all year round. It has a good temperament and may be any solid colour.

Driving pony

With their fast action, Section C ponies are ideal for driving. They are also good riding ponies, can jump well, and are strong enough to carry light adults as well as children.

Welsh Section D

The Section D, or Welsh Cob, was bred from the Welsh Mountain Pony, with crosses to Spanish horses, trotters and Arabs between the 11th and 19th centuries. The Cob was used for all-round farm work and riding, and for pulling carts in cities.

Head looks like a pony's

Neck is strong and arched

Hindquarters are powerful

Legs carry some feather

The Section D stands between 14.2 and 15.2hh (147–157cm) and may be any solid colour. It is famous for its fast, high-stepping trot, is an ideal driving pony, a good jumper, and is also used for riding and trekking.

Fell

This breed of pony is about 2,000 years old. Fell ponies come from Cumbria, England, and have Friesian ancestors. They were used as pack animals to carry lead from the mines to the docks, and often travelled 386km in a week. They were also ridden and driven, and used for farm work and herding.

These ponies are only 14hh (142cm), but they can carry 100kg packs or be ridden by adult riders. They are strong, hardy, sure-footed and energetic. They are always black or dark brown, with only small white markings allowed.

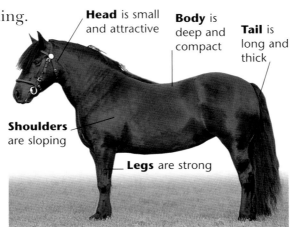

Head is small and attractive

Body is deep and compact

Tail is long and thick

Shoulders are sloping

Legs are strong

Good riding pony

The Fell's sloping shoulders make it more suitable for riding than the Dales pony, and it can be ridden by everyone in the family. It is also used for trekking. The Fell does well in harness and is popular for competition driving.

Dales

This strong and sturdy pony comes from Durham, North Yorkshire and Northumberland, England. It was also used as a pack pony to carry lead across the hills. The breed is about 2,000 years old, and has Welsh Cob and Clydesdale ancestors.

The Dales is more of a harness pony than the Fell. It is taller, more solidly built and has higher knee action. It is about 14.2hh (147cm) and is usually black in colour. The Dales is also used for general riding.

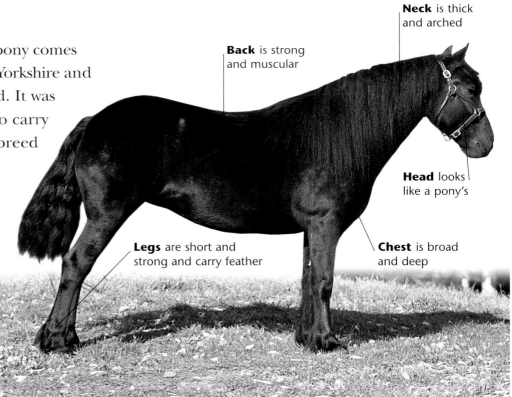

Neck is thick and arched

Back is strong and muscular

Head looks like a pony's

Legs are short and strong and carry feather

Chest is broad and deep

Highland

The Highland has existed in Scotland since the last Ice Age and is the largest of Britain's pony breeds. They were bred for farm work, forestry and deer-stalking, and there were three sizes – the smallest from the islands and the largest from the mainland. Today, there is little difference between the three.

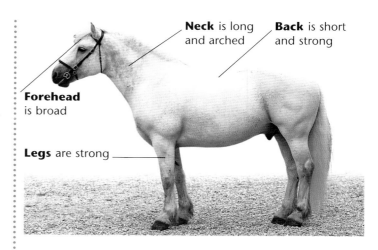

Neck is long and arched

Back is short and strong

Forehead is broad

Legs are strong

Powerfully built and very strong, the Highland looks like some of the ponies that are seen in ancient cave paintings. It often has an eel stripe along its back and zebra markings on its legs. Its shoulders are massive and its feet are hard and tough. It is long-lived, easy to keep and has a docile, gentle nature.

Facts and figures

- **Place of origin**
  Scottish Highlands, UK

- **Height**
  13–14.2hh (132–147cm)

- **Colour**
  Grey, dun, brown, black

- **Uses**
  Riding, trekking, harness

Champion pony
The champion Highland stallion Duart of Glenmuick (right) has the breed's characteristic full mane and tail.

Special mane

The Fjord's mane is dark in the centre and silvery white on the outside. It is cut to stand upright, in a long curve, with the outer hair shorter than at the centre.

Fjord

The Fjord is an ancient breed descended from Przewalski's Horse. It has many characteristics of primitive horses, being dun in colour, with a dorsal stripe and sometimes zebra stripes on its legs. The Fjord is strong and sure-footed, hardy and economical to keep, and has great powers of endurance.

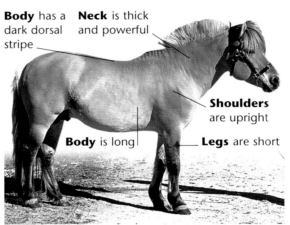

Body has a dark dorsal stripe

Neck is thick and powerful

Shoulders are upright

Body is long

Legs are short

The Vikings used ponies that looked like the Fjord, and shipped them in longboats to Scotland and Iceland. Since ancient times, this pony has been used for work on mountain farms, as well as being a riding and pack pony. The pony stands between 13 and 14.2hh (132–147cm).

Icelandic

Although the Icelandic is only small, people call it a horse. It stands between 12.3 and 13.2hh (130–137cm), but is strong enough to carry an adult for long distances. The Vikings brought these ponies to Iceland, and the breed has been kept pure for 1,000 years. Icelandics are ridden, driven and used for trekking.

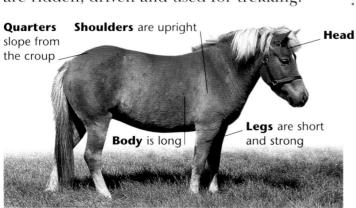

Quarters slope from the croup

Shoulders are upright

Head is large

Body is long

Legs are short and strong

As well as walking, trotting, cantering and galloping, Icelandic ponies can perform a gait called the *skeid*, which is pacing, and the *tölt*, which is a fast, running walk. They take part in competitions for gaited horses.

Outdoor pony

Although the Icelandic winter is harsh, these ponies often live outside in a semi-wild state. This makes them tough and hardy. They are also very sure-footed, moving easily over the rough and mountainous ground of their island home.

Haflinger

These ponies have been bred in the Austrian mountains for over 200 years. All native Haflingers have a brand mark – a letter 'H' and an edelweiss, the national flower of Austria. They were used for all kinds of farm and forestry work, as well as for riding. They are now popular trekking ponies.

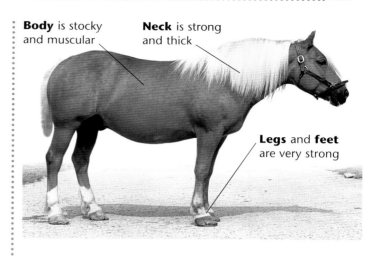

Body is stocky and muscular

Neck is strong and thick

Legs and **feet** are very strong

As well as being sturdy and tough, Haflingers usually live for a long time. They start working at four years old, and may continue until the age of 40 – almost twice as long as the average horse. Haflingers have a docile temperament and are easy to handle.

Facts and figures

- **Place of origin**
  Austrian Tyrol, Europe

- **Height**
  13.1–14.2hh (135–147cm)

- **Colour**
  Chestnut or palomino

- **Uses**
  Riding, trekking, harness

Sleigh ride
Haflingers pull sleighs in winter. Their harness may be decorated for Christmas.

New breeds of the USA

Some stallions produce foals that have similar characteristics to their sire, or father. This quality is called 'prepotency', and horses that have it may be used to start new breeds. Once a breed is established, a stud book is set up in which horses that meet the breed's standards are registered.

Body is well-proportioned

Neck is long, arched and graceful

Head shows pony's Spanish ancestry

Feet are strong

Rocky Mountain

This pony may be the world's most recent breed, as the stud book registrations only began in 1986. Although there are other colours, the favourite is a unique chocolate brown with a flaxen mane and tail. The Rocky Mountain is sometimes called a horse because of its height. It is hardy, and can survive in harsh winter weather.

Ears are exceptionally long

Show driving
The American Shetland, driven to a show carriage, is a popular attraction in the USA. This pony also races in harness, and some types are ridden and jumped in the show ring.

American Shetland

This pony is very different from the Shetland of the British Isles. The breed was developed in the 1880s by crossing lightly built Shetlands with Hackney Ponies, and the result is a Hackney-type show harness pony.

Mane and **tail** are long and thick

Body is long and narrow

Head is more like a horse's than a pony's

Head and neck carriage are like those of the Hackney Pony

Ponies often stand with legs stretched out

Special gait
Although this graceful pony is cantering, the characteristic action of the Rocky Mountain is pacing. In this gait, both legs on the same side move together. The Rocky Mountain can reach speeds of up to 25km/h when pacing.

Facts and figures

Rocky Mountain Pony

- **Height**
  14.2–15hh (147–152cm)

- **Colour**
  Chocolate, with flaxen mane and tail, plus others

American Shetland

- **Height**
  Up to 11.2hh (117cm)

- **Colour**
  Any solid colour

Pony of the Americas

- **Height**
  11.2–13hh (117–132cm)

- **Colour**
  Markings are the same as the Appaloosa

Pony of the Americas

This breed was started in Iowa in the 1950s when a Shetland pony was crossed with an Appaloosa. The foal that they produced was the first of the breed. Ponies of the Americas are small and stocky, and have the traditional Appaloosa markings. These ponies are docile and good-natured.

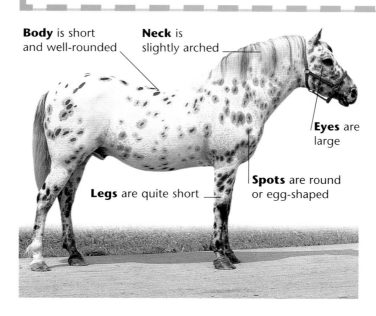

Body is short and well-rounded

Neck is slightly arched

Eyes are large

Legs are quite short

Spots are round or egg-shaped

On the leading rein
These ponies are small and easy to handle, so they are good for children who are learning to ride. First lessons are often on a leading rein.

Caspian

The Caspian is possibly the oldest breed of horse or pony that exists, and it may be the ancestor of the Arab. Since prehistoric times it has lived near the southern coast of the Caspian Sea, in what is now Iran. In the mid-20th century, the breed was rediscovered, and these ponies are now bred in Europe, America, Australia and New Zealand.

The Caspian looks more like a miniature horse than a pony. It is lightly built, has a fine, silky coat, mane and tail, and is very fast for its size. The Caspian stands 10 to 12hh (102–122cm), and it is usually bay or chestnut in colour.

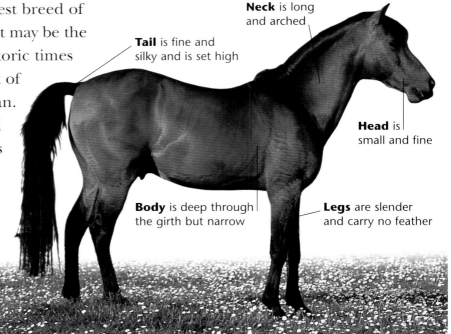

Neck is long and arched

Tail is fine and silky and is set high

Head is small and fine

Body is deep through the girth but narrow

Legs are slender and carry no feather

Chincoteague and Assateague

Chincoteague and Assateague are islands off the coast of Virginia, USA, where these small wild ponies have lived since the 16th century. They may be the descendants of Barb horses that were once shipwrecked there.

Quarters slope sharply from the croup

Back is short

Head may be large and plain

These ponies have lived on islands for hundreds of years so they have not been crossed with other breeds. They are about 12hh (122cm) and may be any colour. They are often skewbald or piebald (see Pinto page 52).

Island ponies

Once a year, the Assateague ponies are taken across to Chincoteague island, where the young animals are sold. These ponies are strong-willed and can be difficult to handle, but some are used for riding.

Basuto

This pony is named after the area of South Africa where it was developed between the 17th and 19th centuries. It has Arab, Barb and Thoroughbred ancestors. The Basuto often had to endure harsh conditions, so this breed is strong and tough. The British used Basuto ponies during the Boer War.

Head may have Arab features

Neck is thin

Back is long

Shoulders are upright

Feet are hard

The Basuto is about 14.2hh (147cm). It has great stamina, and can be ridden every day for many miles. This makes the Basuto a popular trekking pony. It is usually brown, bay, grey or chestnut in colour.

Herding pony

Farmers in Lesotho, Africa, use Basuto ponies for herding animals, as well as for riding round their land. In the past, these ponies have been raced, and also used by the army and for polo. They are popular general riding ponies in southern Africa.

Boer

The Boer pony developed in the 19th century in South Africa, and has similar ancestors to the Basuto. Most Boer ponies did not have to endure such harsh conditions as the Basuto, so this breed is often taller and of better quality. The Boer is known as the 'Boerperd' in its native country. It is found in the north-eastern part of South Africa, where it is used as an all-round farm horse.

Neck is long and carried high

Expression is alert

Pasterns are long and sloping

Body is narrow

Legs are long and slender

The Boer's height ranges from 13.3 to 15.3hh (140–160cm) and it may be any solid colour, including palomino. Some Boers are five-gaited, and can perform the slow gait and rack as well as the walk, trot and canter. They are popular endurance horses.

Australian

Ponies were first brought to Australia in the early 19th century, and in the 20th century, the Australian pony officially became a breed. Its ancestors include the Hackney, the Shetland, the Arab, the Thoroughbred and the Welsh Mountain Pony (Section A), which it closely resembles.

The Australian pony stands between 12 and 14hh (122–142cm) and is an attractive animal. Its action is free and level, and it is good-natured and easy to handle. This breed may be any solid colour and in Australia it is a popular riding and show pony.

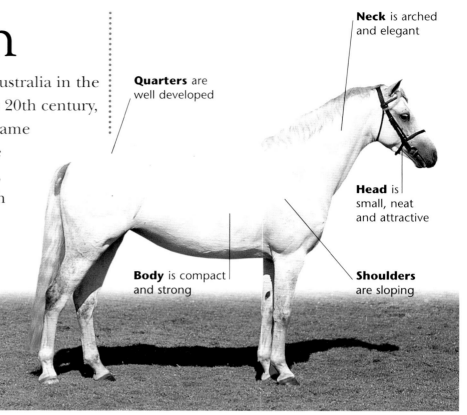

Neck is arched and elegant

Quarters are well developed

Head is small, neat and attractive

Body is compact and strong

Shoulders are sloping

Falabella

The little Falabella is named after the family who created it near Buenos Aires, Argentina, in the early 20th century. They crossed tiny Shetland ponies with a small Thoroughbred, and kept breeding from the smallest ponies produced. Falabellas are 'inbred' so they are not strong, and need looking after carefully. They are not ridden, though they are sometimes driven. Falabellas are mostly kept as pets.

Tiny foal

Falabella foals are only about 4hh (41cm), but they grow quickly. When the mother is pregnant, she carries her foal for 13 months, which is two months longer than other horses and ponies.

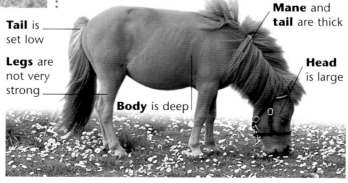

Tail is set low

Legs are not very strong

Body is deep

Mane and **tail** are thick

Head is large

Falabellas are about 7 to 8.2hh (71–86cm) and may be any colour. People think of them as miniature horses rather than small ponies, as they have fine bones and slender legs. They are clever and friendly, and make good pets.

Shetland

The Shetland is the smallest of Britain's mountain and moorland ponies. It has lived in the bleak Shetland Islands, north-east of Scotland, for about 10,000 years. The harsh climate and poor grazing have made it very hardy. For its size, the Shetland is probably the strongest of all horses and ponies.

Body is deep and compact

Tail is full

Head is neat

Legs are short

Shetlands are measured in inches, not in hands, and are up to 42in (107cm) high. They can be any colour. They are used as children's riding ponies, and in harness, where they are especially good at scurry driving.

Tough ponies

These ponies can survive in the snow and strong winds of their island home. They grow thick coats and can live on very little food. Their small size means they can find shelter more easily than larger ponies.

Hackney

The Hackney Pony is a smaller, pony-like version of the Hackney Horse. The breed was produced in the 19th century from Fell and Welsh ponies and the Yorkshire Trotter. These early ponies were very hardy, and today's Hackneys are strong and tough, with great stamina. Hackneys have a high neck carriage, short, compact bodies and long, powerful legs. They can be 12.2 to 14hh (127–142cm), and are brown, bay or black.

Spectacular action

The Hackney's high-stepping action is a spectacular sight, and produces much applause in the show ring. About 100 years ago, these ponies could be seen on city streets, where they were used by tradesmen delivering goods. Today, they are almost always show harness ponies.

Keeping
a pony

Keeping and looking after a pony is
a serious commitment. It is hard
work, and takes up a lot of your time.
It is also exciting, rewarding – and great fun!

Providing company

Horses and ponies are herd animals and do not like being on their own. They are happiest when living with other horses and ponies, but if this is not possible, then the company of other animals is a good substitute. If you have to keep a pony on his own, visit him frequently and make him feel he is part of family life.

Human contact

Ponies like human company and will always appreciate your visits, though you may not be important enough to them to stop them grazing! Take care they do not tread on your feet as they walk forwards. If you do offer titbits, make sure there are enough to go round all the ponies in the group.

Ponies always enjoy a treat, but they will be pleased to see you even if you visit empty-handed as long as you talk to them and pat them.

Animal companionship

Once they get to know each other and realize they are part of a group that lives together, most animals become friends. Horses and ponies get on well with a variety of animals, from cats and dogs to farm stock.

Although one horse or pony in a group is always dominant, two horses kept together usually become firm friends.

Horses and cats get on well. A cat is a good companion for a pony in the stable or out.

A friendly goat is good company for a lonely horse or pony, as are farm animals such as cattle and sheep.

Regular exercise

If a pony is kept in a stable he must be exercised every day. If it is not possible to ride him, then he should be turned out in the field for a while, or lunged. Exercise keeps the pony fit. His circulation, heart and lungs function better, and his bones and muscles are kept strong and healthy.

What a pony needs

Apony needs food and water, shelter from the weather, regular exercise and companionship. In his natural state, all these things are part of the life that he leads. But when we domesticate horses and ponies and make them work for us, they depend on us to fulfil all these needs. We owe it to them to do this as well as we possibly can.

Some form of shelter

A pony that lives out in a field needs some kind of shelter from sun and flies in summer, and rain, wind and snow in winter. Trees and thick hedges provide a certain amount of protection, but a specially built field shelter is the best solution if it is possible.

Grazing in the field

Every pony should have access to good grazing for at least part of each day. This is his natural way of life. Giving him the freedom to graze, move from place to place, roll and occasionally gallop around, helps to keep him calm.

A suitable stable

If the pony is to be stabled, the building must meet certain requirements. The doorway should be high enough so he cannot bang his head. The stable should be light, with plenty of ventilation. It should have good drainage, so that the bedding stays as dry as possible.

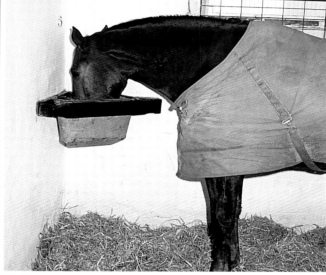

Feeding routine

A stabled pony needs regular feeding. The amount of food he needs depends on the individual and the amount of work he is being asked to do, but all stabled ponies need hay to replace the grass they would eat if they lived out in a field and grazed.

Stable bedding

The purpose of bedding is to provide a warm, dry, comfortable floor covering on which a horse or pony can lie down without knocking or injuring himself. It also takes some of the strain off the legs when a horse has to stand for long periods on a hard surface. Many different types are available. Whatever kind you choose, the bedding should be at least 15cm deep.

Straw is the dried stalks of wheat, barley or oats. It is cheap to buy, but some ponies like eating it and it can give them colic.

Aubiose is made from hemp. Sold in vacuum-packed bales, it is useful for horses and ponies who have dust allergies. It is expensive to buy.

Rubber matting is very expensive but saves time on mucking out. You need to use some bedding on top of it to soak up the wet.

Wood shavings are also sold vacuum-packed. Dust-extracted, they are good for horses and ponies with breathing problems.

Shredded paper is cheap, but some ponies are allergic to the ink in it. It is heavy to lift and unpleasant to handle when it is wet.

Far to walk
You may have to carry a field-kept pony's tack quite a distance.

Ways to keep a pony

You can keep a pony out in a field, in a stable, or partly in and partly out. Looking after a stabled pony is hard work and takes up a lot of time. It also costs more than keeping a pony in a field, but it is very convenient. A field-kept pony requires less looking after, but preparing him for riding takes longer. Many people think the ideal system is to stable ponies at night in winter and during the day in summer, and let them live out the rest of the time.

Winter field

In winter, fields can become very muddy and your pony may be wet and dirty most of the time. This is bad for his feet and legs. But field-kept ponies are less likely to suffer from coughs and breathing problems than stabled ponies.

Preparing for a ride

It is easy to prepare a stabled pony for riding. But before you can ride a field-kept pony you must walk to the field, catch him and then get him clean enough to tack up.

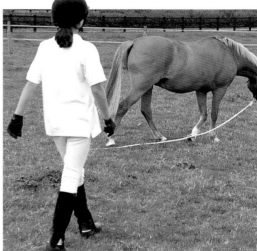

Catching a pony

Some ponies are difficult to catch, and some may try to pull away once caught. A trailing rope can be dangerous, so try not to let it go. It may be better to lead a difficult pony in a bridle.

Regular feeding routine

When ponies are kept in stables they need feeding at regular times. Whether or not they have hard feed (page 93), they need hay fed in a haynet several times a day to give them the bulk food that grazing would provide if they lived out.

Mucking out

When you keep a pony in a stable, you have to muck it out thoroughly at least once a day, as well as removing droppings at regular intervals. This takes a lot of time and can be very hard work.

A stabled pony is entirely dependent on you for food and water.

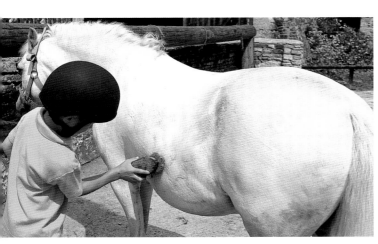

Removing mud and stains

A stabled pony needs just a quick brush over before exercise to make him look presentable. This is called quartering (page 99). With a field-kept pony you must remove all the mud stuck to his coat. It is especially important to remove mud where the tack fits, or it may rub and cause sores.

Carrying water to the field

If the field does not have a trough that fills automatically, you will have to carry water to it every day. In warm weather, and if there are several ponies in the field, this can mean many trips to and fro with buckets.

American barn stabling

Many livery yards and riding schools now use American barn stabling. A long barn is divided into individual loose boxes with a central aisle. It is convenient in bad weather, but there can be problems with ventilation.

Where to keep a pony

If you are a new owner it is a good idea to keep your pony at a livery yard where you will have knowledgeable people to help you. Types of livery, and their charges, vary. Some riding schools charge less if they can use your pony for lessons. You may be able to rent a field and stable from a farmer, or be lucky enough to keep your pony at home.

Traditional loose boxes

Each loose box opens directly on to the yard, so the horses can see what is going on. An overhanging roof gives some protection from sun and rain to both the horses and the people working in and around the stables.

Planning a conversion

You may have a garage or outbuilding at home that can be turned into a stable. In most areas, your parents will have to apply for planning permission to change the use of the building, and they will have to submit plans to the local council. This can all take a long time.

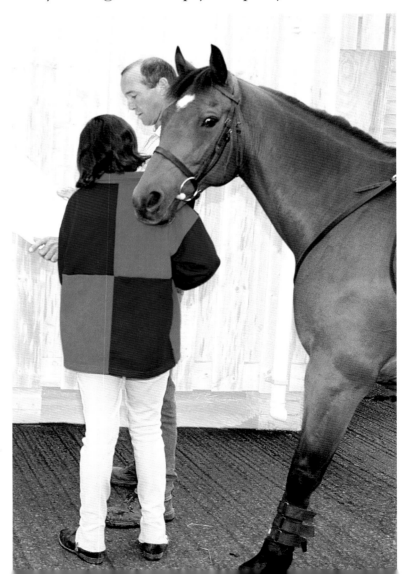

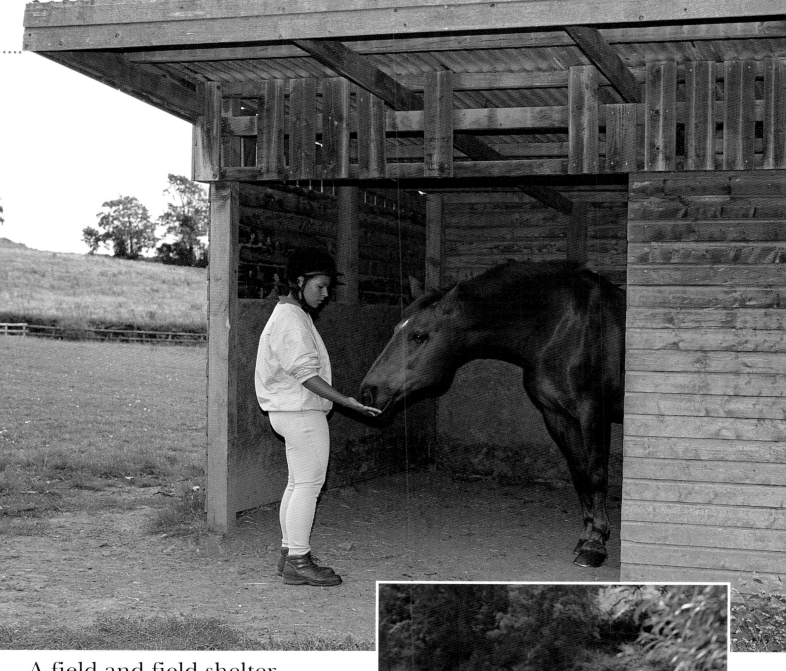

A field and field shelter

If you only have a field in which to keep your pony, try to make sure there is some kind of shelter. This will protect your pony from the weather, as well as giving you a base in which you can put your belongings, groom the pony, tack him up, and feed him in winter. Do not leave tack in the shelter.

A farmer's field

A local farmer may let you rent a field and possibly a stable, too, though many do not like having horses on their land. If you do find one who is willing, it can be very useful because he will probably be able to supply you with hay and may even let you ride in some of his fields.

A stable of your own

If you want to keep a pony in your own stable at home, you need to plan well beforehand. The stable does not have to be perfect, or even conventional, but it must meet certain basic requirements and be safe and comfortable for the pony.

A converted building

You may be lucky enough to have a building at home that you can use as a stable. It must be in good condition, with a weatherproof roof and a sound floor. It must also be well ventilated.

A ready-made stable

You can buy a wooden stable as a kit and have it assembled at your home. You will need some kind of level, solid base on which to stand it. This will probably mean laying a concrete slab. You need to consider the site you will use carefully before you go ahead.

Planning a stable yard

If you are considering keeping a pony at home, remember you will need more than just a building in which to house it. Although you may only be planning to use one loose box, you will have to find space for storing feed, hay and bedding, and the latter two take up a lot of room. You must reserve a corner not too near the house for the muck heap. Tack and rugs must be kept somewhere, and if you do not have a paddock, you will have to find a field for a daily turn-out.

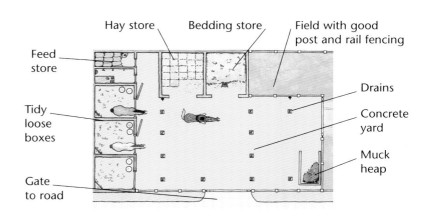

Hay store • Bedding store • Field with good post and rail fencing • Feed store • Tidy loose boxes • Gate to road • Drains • Concrete yard • Muck heap

A stable's requirements

When you are planning your stable, consider what it needs. First of all it must be large enough – about three metres by three metres for a pony. The doorway and ceiling must be high enough for him not to bang his head if he throws it up in the air. You will need a water supply nearby. Electricity is useful, but not absolutely essential. If you do have it, you must install light bulbs and switches where the pony cannot reach them.

Tying ring
It is useful to have tying rings both inside and outside the stable for tying up the pony and for hanging a haynet.

Double doors
The open top half of the door allows the pony to look out. It should always be left open for ventilation.

Automatic waterer
This needs to be plumbed in, but it will save a lot of time and effort carrying water buckets.

Hopper windows
The top half of the windows should open inwards to let in air but not rain, and the glass should be protected by grilles.

Manger
You can feed a pony or horse from a bowl or bucket standing on the floor, but a manger is less likely to become soiled.

Door bolts
Some ponies can undo the top bolts on their doors. A bolt with a lockable end prevents them from doing this.

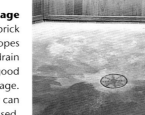

Good drainage
A concrete or brick floor that slopes gently to a drain will provide good stable drainage. An earth floor can also be used.

Kick bolt
A foot-operated kick bolt on the lower part of the door saves having to bend down – useful when carrying things.

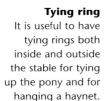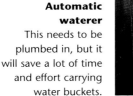

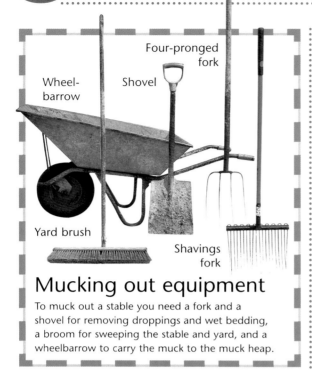

Four-pronged
fork

Wheel-
barrow

Shovel

Yard brush

Shavings
fork

Mucking out equipment

To muck out a stable you need a fork and a
shovel for removing droppings and wet bedding,
a broom for sweeping the stable and yard, and a
wheelbarrow to carry the muck to the muck heap.

Stable management

Stable management means the organization and carrying out of all the tasks that are centred round the stable. A large part of stable management is the daily routine of mucking out, feeding and watering, as well as keeping the stable and yard clean and tidy. Other jobs include the maintenance of equipment and checking feed and bedding stores.

Mucking out a pony's stable

A pony's stable needs a thorough mucking out once a
day – removing the droppings and wet bedding – and
skipping out – just removing the droppings – several times
a day. The process is much the same for straw or shavings.
Some people use a deep litter system, in which only the
droppings are removed daily and fresh bedding is added.

Clearing up
Sweep any remaining
muck and wet bits of
bedding into a pile in the
middle of the floor and
use the shovel to put it
all into the wheelbarrow.
Continue sweeping until
the floor is clean.

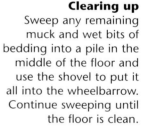

1 First remove
all the obvious
droppings on the
surface with the
shavings fork and put
them in the barrow.

2 When you have
done this, toss the
shavings to the sides of
the stable, removing any
droppings that fall out
of them as you do so.

3 Once you have
removed the top
shavings, those that
remain on the floor will
be wet. Scoop them up
with the shavings fork.

4 Now the dry bedding
is stacked round the
sides and most of the
wet has been removed,
you can sweep the floor
and shovel up the muck.

The bedding store

Shavings and straw bales must be stored somewhere. Straw must be stacked under cover, preferably in a hay barn, where air can circulate round it and prevent it from going musty. Shavings can be stacked outside, if possible under a waterproof cover.

Clean water

Horses and ponies should have access to clean water at all times. Whenever you visit the stable, check the bucket to see if it needs topping up. If the water is soiled, throw it away and rinse the bucket out well before refilling it. Every few days, scrub out the water bucket to keep it clean.

A tidy muck heap

Try to keep your muck heap tidy. Ideally, you should divide it into three sections: one that you are using to tip the muck on each day, one that you are leaving to rot down, and one that has already rotted down to be used on the garden or disposed of elsewhere.

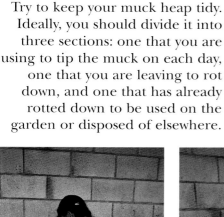

Water buckets are usually made of plastic or rubber.

5 If possible, leave the floor to dry and air for a while before pulling back the shavings to lay the bed. Bank up the shavings round the walls.

6 You may not always need to add new shavings, but when you do, open the bale carefully, cutting the tape with scissors or a special safety yard knife that has a recessed blade.

7 Shavings are very tightly packed in their bales. It is often easiest to use the four-pronged fork to prise them out if you do not need to add a whole new bale to the bedding.

Choosing a field

A field suitable for grazing by horses and ponies should be level and well drained. It needs some form of shade and shelter, such as trees, hedges or a field shelter; secure, safe fencing; a clean water supply; safe access from the road; and a properly hung gate that can be locked if necessary. The grazing and hedges should be free from all kinds of poisonous plants.

Good fencing

Wooden post and rail is the best kind of fencing for horses and ponies, but it is expensive. Hedges with gaps in them and crumbling stone walls can be reinforced by a taut strand of electrified tape. Electric fencing works well if you keep it clear of the ground and check the supply regularly.

Good grazing

Horses and ponies thrive on a mixture of grasses, such as rye, timothy and meadow fescue, with some beneficial herbs and weeds such as dandelion, chicory and yarrow. Lush pasture fertilized with nitrates is not suitable for horses. The grazing must be properly managed.

Poisonous plants

You should check any field in which you are going to keep a pony for poisonous plants. Any you find should be dug up and burned. If the field is near a garden, check that the pony cannot reach plants such as rhododendron, laburnum, privet or other evergreen hedges. Most evergreens are poisonous.

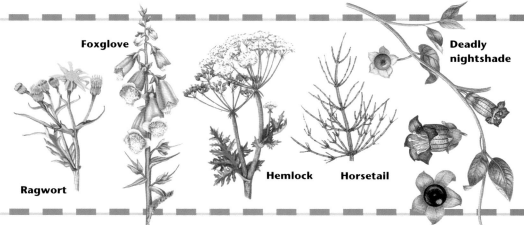

Foxglove

Deadly nightshade

Hemlock   Horsetail

Ragwort

Water supply

A stream is not ideal because it may be polluted. A water trough that fills automatically is very useful, or you may have to use buckets. Both the trough and the buckets need scrubbing out regularly to remove the algae that build up.

Secure locks
Unless the field is well supervised, it is as well to keep the gate locked as a precaution against theft.

Safe gate

A properly hung and well-maintained gate that does not sag on its hinges, drag on the ground as you open and close it, or swing back and hit you as you go through, ensures you can lead your pony into the field safely. The gate may be made of wood or metal.

Signs of a bad field

A field that is covered in droppings and has more weeds than grass, with broken fencing and a gate held in place with string, is not suitable for a pony.

Uneven grazing
Tussocks of coarse grass surrounded by bare pasture usually mean that the field has been over-grazed. It needs topping and resting before being used again for horses or ponies.

Poached field
Poached means that the field is badly cut up and muddy. A poorly drained field with too many animals on it in winter quickly becomes poached, and is no use for grazing.

Too many droppings
A field covered in piles of droppings needs clearing and resting. The droppings kill the grass and contain many worm eggs. Grazing round these areas reinfests a horse.

Barbed wire fencing
Barbed wire should never be used for fencing where horses and ponies are kept. Many have been injured by it. The wire is especially dangerous if it is rusty or sagging.

Yew

Oak (acorns)

Rhododendron

Laburnum

Bracken

Laurel

Looking after a pony's field

A pony's field needs a lot of attention to stay in good condition. Horses and ponies tend to graze parts of a field until they are bare, leaving tussocks of coarse grass and weeds untouched. Putting other animals in the field evens out the grazing, but it may also need spreading with fertilizer or lime, and rolling in the spring if it gets very churned up in winter.

Pulling up ragwort

Ragwort is a tall, poisonous plant with small, yellow, daisy-like flowers and ragged leaves. You should check a pony's paddock regularly for ragwort and pull

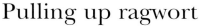

or dig up any immediately. All traces of the plant should be destroyed. Put salt in the hole left after pulling it up to kill any remaining roots.

Removing droppings

Leaving droppings around not only damages the grass, but also encourages parasitic worms to breed. In a small field you should remove droppings every day with a shovel and a wheelbarrow or skip. This may not be practical if horses or ponies graze a large field, so the area should be harrowed instead to break up and scatter the droppings. The sun will then dry them out and kill off any worm eggs.

Grazing in rotation

Grazing a pony paddock with sheep or cattle is one way to stop worm eggs developing, because the worms can live only in horses' and ponies' digestive systems. If possible, a field should be grazed in rotation by horses, cattle and sheep.

Topping a field

Once or twice each summer, a field needs topping, which is rather like mowing a lawn. A tractor pulls a machine that cuts down weeds such as docks, nettles and thistles, as well as the long, coarse grasses. This helps to stunt the weeds' growth and prevents them from scattering seeds. It also encourages new grass shoots to flourish, which provide more nourishing grazing.

Removing stones

Small stones can get lodged in a horse's or pony's feet and cause lameness. Large stones can be dangerous if horses or ponies gallop round a field, causing them to stumble, sprain tendons or even fall. It is a good idea to remove as many stones from your pony's field as you can.

Clearing rubbish

If a field is near a road, litter such as string (left) and plastic (right) may blow or be thrown into it. Plastic bags can kill a pony if eaten, and cans and glass bottles can cause severe cuts. String can become entangled round a horse's legs and also cause problems if eaten. You should check a field daily and remove any litter you find.

Turning out and catching

Turning out means putting a horse or pony out in a field. It is better to remove his headcollar to avoid any possibility of it getting entangled in fencing or hedges, but sometimes headcollars are left on ponies that are difficult to catch. If your pony gets excited at the thought of joining his friends in the field, try to keep him calm.

Turning out a horse or pony

As you lead your pony towards the field, other horses or ponies already there may gather inquisitively round the gate. If this happens, ask a helper to open the gate for you and shoo them quietly away so that you can take the pony into the field safely.

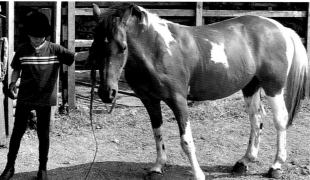

1 Lead the pony a few metres into the field after closing the gate behind you. Turn him round to face the gate and undo the buckle on the headcollar.

2 Slip the headcollar off his head gently and let him walk quietly away. If he gets excited and tries to whip round and gallop off, make sure you keep well out of his way.

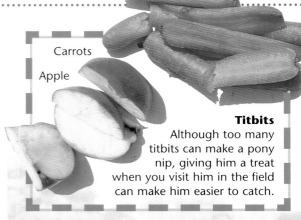

Carrots

Apple

Titbits
Although too many titbits can make a pony nip, giving him a treat when you visit him in the field can make him easier to catch.

Leading a pony

Ponies are usually led on the left-hand side. Hold the rope so that your right hand is near the pony's head with the palm facing down, and your left hand is near the end of the rope. Look straight ahead and walk level with the pony's shoulder.

Keeping hold of a pony

If the pony misbehaves, bring your right hand down to the end of the rope near your left hand. Try your best not to let go, but bring the pony round you in a circle. Never wrap the rope round your hands. If he pulls away, he will drag you after him.

Catching a horse or pony

Some horses and ponies are easier to catch than others. Approach a difficult horse with the headcollar behind your back and your hand outstretched holding a titbit or a bucket of pony nuts. If he runs away, do not chase him. Wait for him to come to you.

1 Walk towards the horse's shoulder from the front, holding out a titbit in your hand so that he can see it.

2 Give him the titbit and quickly slip the headcollar rope round his neck before he has time to move away.

3 Put the headcollar over the horse's nose, still keeping the rope round his neck in case he decides to wander off.

4 Reach under his jaw with your right hand and take hold of the headpiece firmly. Pass it over the top of the horse's head. Get hold of the headcollar's cheekpiece with your other hand.

5 Fasten the buckle of the headpiece so that it fits correctly – not too tight or too loose. Tuck the end of the strap through the buckle to keep it tidy and out of the way. You can then lead the horse in from the field.

Feeding a pony

A pony's natural food is grass. He must eat a lot, taken in a little at a time, to provide nourishment. When we replace grass with hay and other food, we must try to copy this pattern.

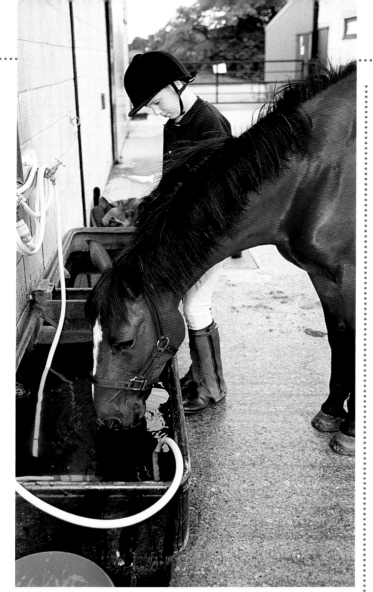

The rules of feeding

Horses' and ponies' stomachs are small and their intestines large. They need small quantities of food at a time, but a lot overall. This is how they eat bulk food such as grass or hay. But with hard feed (see page 93) it is important that they do not get too much food in their stomachs at once.

Plenty of clean water

Clean water should always be available to a horse or pony. If, for some reason, it is not possible to allow him free access to water, then offer it to him at regular intervals before feeding. Watering after food can cause digestive problems such as colic.

Feeding rules

Feed little and often, rather than giving large feeds.

Only feed fresh food.

Match the amount of food to the work the pony does.

Do not exercise a pony immediately after feeding.

Introduce new foods gradually to a pony's diet.

Feed plenty of bulk food, such as good meadow hay.

Allow the pony to graze in the field for part of each day.

Feed a stabled pony something succulent, such as carrots or turnips.

Feed at regular times each day of the week.

Keep the manger clean.

A haynet keeps hay off the floor.

Regular feeds

It is best to give a pony hard feed rations in several small feeds evenly spaced during the day. Work out a routine that suits you and stick to it. Ponies do not understand the difference between a weekday and a weekend – they expect their food to appear at the same time every day.

Different types of feed

Horse and pony feed can be divided into two main types. Bulk feed – grass and hay – forms the major part of the diet. A pony may manage on that alone. If he works hard, he may need up to 30 per cent of his rations in the form of hard feed – also called concentrates.

Filling a haynet

Feeding hay on the floor is wasteful as the hay gets trampled and soiled. To fill a haynet, open it as wide as possible. Tear a slice of hay off the bale, pull it apart and push it into the centre of the haynet. You can get a rough idea of how much you are feeding by counting the number of slices you put in each time.

How much hay?
To be sure exactly how much you are feeding, weigh the filled haynet.

Tying a quick-release knot

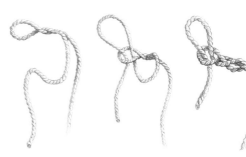

Make a loop in the rope and put it through the tying ring. Twist the base of the loop several times.

Make a second loop in the loose end of the rope, and then push this through the first loop you have made.

Tighten the knot by pulling on the attached end of the rope. Undo the knot by pulling the loose end.

Hanging a haynet

The haynet should be tied up quite high to prevent the horse from pawing at it and getting his foot stuck in it. Using a quick-release knot makes it easy to undo when it is empty.

1 Put the string of the haynet through the tying ring in the stable. Pull on the string to raise the haynet to the right height.

2 Loop the string through the rope mesh near the bottom of the haynet and take it back up to the tying ring.

3 Put the end of the string through the tying ring again and secure the haynet firmly with a quick-release knot.

Types of hard feed

Oats can make ponies unmanageable so it may be better to feed barley instead. Most hard feeds are best mixed with chaff (chopped hay and straw). Bran is used in mashes. Maize should be fed sparingly; sugar beet must be soaked before feeding. Pony nuts and coarse mixes are easy to feed.

Pony nuts

Coarse mix

Flaked maize

Bran

Dry sugar beet

Micronized flaked barley

Soaked sugar beet

Chaff

Bruised oats

How to store feed

Feed must be kept in a cool, dry place and protected from rats and mice. In large stables, sacks of hard feed are emptied into metal feed bins, but for one pony, plastic dustbins make good substitutes. Hay must be kept in a dry barn where air can circulate round it.

Supplements and treats

All horses and ponies need salt, which can be provided by a mineral lick. In winter, feeding a little cod liver oil supplies essential vitamins. Ponies appreciate carrots, swedes and turnips both as treats and as winter feed. Apples are always very popular, but feeding too many can cause colic.

Mineral lick
Ponies enjoy licking and gnawing at mineral blocks both out in the field and in the stable.

Vegetable oils
Ponies need some fat in their diet and this can be provided by oils such as sunflower oil. About one tablespoonful can be added to a feed.

A diet for your pony

Horses and ponies may be 'good doers' or 'bad doers'. This means they can do well or even get fat on little food, or stay thin while eating a lot. An experienced horse-keeper will be able to work out a diet for a difficult horse or pony. With most ponies, it is better to be cautious about feeding, and if in doubt, give less rather than more. It is not kind to let a pony get overweight.

Working out your pony's weight

You can check your pony's weight with a weighband – a kind of tape measure. You pass the weighband round the pony's girth, and as well as reading the measurement, you can also read off his weight. You may need an assistant on the other side of the pony to check that the band is in the right position. You can also weigh the pony on a weighbridge.

Too thin or too fat?

Although they may both be the same height, a stockily built pony, such as a Highland, will carry much more weight than a thoroughbred type. So you have to assess a pony's fatness according to his type. It is important for the pony's health that he should be the right weight. A thin pony feels the cold. He uses his feed to keep warm, and may have little energy left for working. A fat pony puts a strain on his joints and heart.

A thin pony
If you can see a pony's ribs, if his hip bones stick out and his head looks too big for his neck, he is too thin. This may be the result of teeth problems, worms or lack of food.

A fat pony
When you cannot feel a pony's ribs or spine, and he has thick pads of fat over his shoulders and a large round belly, he is too fat. Fat ponies are prone to illnesses such as laminitis.

The perfect weight
A pony's outline should be smooth and rounded, without any obvious fat. You should not be able to see his bones, but you should be able to feel them if you prod with a finger.

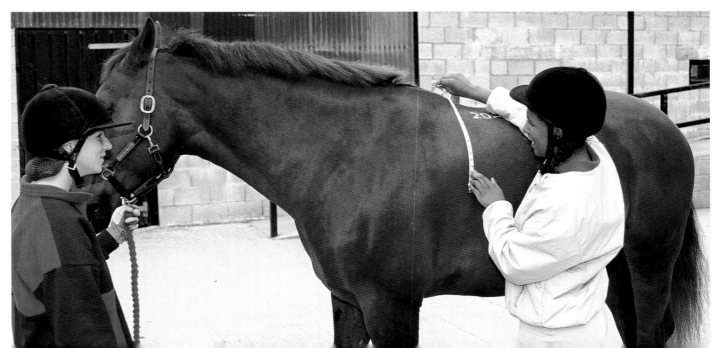

Measuring out

The only way you can be sure exactly how much food your pony is eating is to measure it out. Work out how much food he needs, by multiplying his weight by 2.5 and dividing the answer by 200, and write it down. Decide what proportion of this should be hard feed and measure it out for each feed.

Starvation paddock

Lush summer grazing can be too rich for some ponies, that become overweight and risk getting laminitis. Although it may sound cruel, they are best kept on an almost bare paddock, where they have to work hard to get grass to eat. An alternative is to stable them for most of the time and only let them out to graze for short periods.

Using a bucket muzzle

This is another way of stopping grazing ponies from eating too much. The muzzle has large holes at the front for breathing, and small holes underneath that allow a certain amount of grazing and let the pony drink. The muzzle is held in place by a head strap, which you thread through the rings on the headcollar.

Soaking a haynet

Ponies that suffer from dust allergies and have breathing difficulties are best fed hay that has been soaked in a tub of water for a short while. A plastic dustbin is ideal. Filled haynets can be very heavy when wet, so take care not to strain your back when lifting them out.

Weighing hay

It is a good idea to weigh filled haynets so you know exactly how much hay the pony is being fed. You can buy special spring balances, which you can hang in the feed room or on a gate, designed to weigh a filled haynet. If you are feeding your pony soaked hay, weigh it before you soak it.

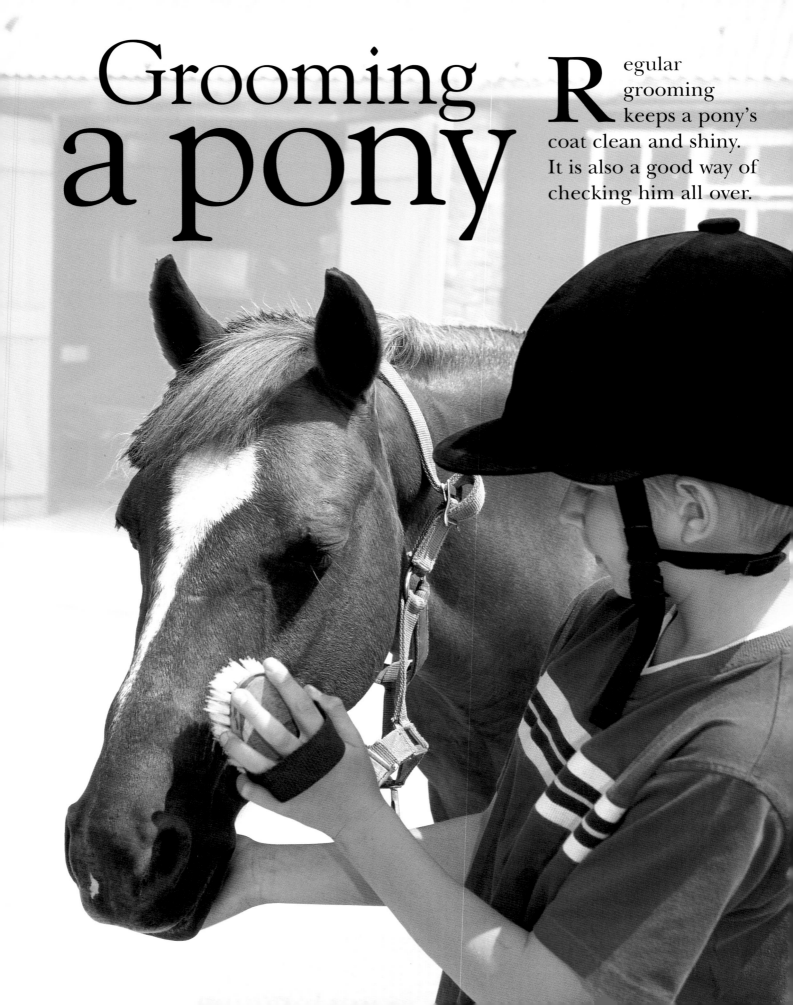

Grooming a pony

R egular grooming keeps a pony's coat clean and shiny. It is also a good way of checking him all over.

Grooming equipment

Grooming means cleaning the pony's coat, tidying his mane and tail, picking out his feet, and keeping his eyes, nostrils, muzzle and dock area clean. Each of these tasks needs a particular piece of equipment. Using the right equipment for each part of the grooming process enables you to carry out the work more efficiently.

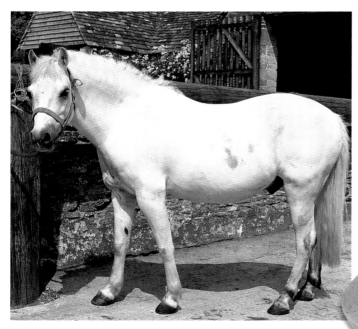

Why do I need to groom?

A fit, hard-working pony needs grooming every day to keep his skin clean and in good condition. But all ponies need brushing over regularly to remove dried mud and stable stains and keep the mane and tail tidy. This not only makes them look better, the ponies are also more pleasant to handle, and you and your clothes will stay cleaner.

Parts of the grooming kit

Ideally, you need all the different grooming aids shown here, but you could start with a few and build up gradually. To begin with, a dandy brush, body brush, metal curry comb, hoof pick and sponges are the most important things.

A dandy brush has stiff bristles and is used for removing dried mud.

A body brush has short bristles, designed to remove dust and grease from the pony's coat and skin.

A plastic or rubber curry comb is used to remove mud, loose hairs and stains.

A metal curry comb is pulled across a body brush to clean it. It is not for use on the pony.

A hoof pick, which may have a brush attached, is used to remove dirt and stones from the feet.

A water brush is used damp to lay the pony's mane and tail in place as a finishing touch.

A mane comb is mostly used when pulling the mane and tail, to tidy them, and to separate the hairs before plaiting.

Hoof grease or oil is applied to the feet with a brush to give a smart finish for a special occasion.

One sponge is used to clean the eyes, nose and muzzle, the other to clean the dock area.

A stable rubber is a cloth used at the end of the grooming routine to remove any remaining traces of dust.

Grooming routines

A pony that lives out should only be brushed over lightly with a dandy brush to keep it tidy. A hard-working, stabled pony needs to be groomed thoroughly each day to keep its skin in good condition. Both the dandy and body brushes are used in the direction of the hair of the pony's coat.

Clean the body brush on the metal curry comb after every three or four strokes.

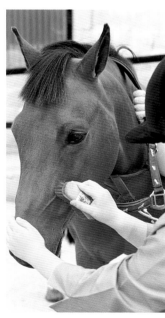

1 For a thorough grooming, first tie up the pony. Starting at the top of his neck on the left-hand side, groom him all over using the body brush.

2 Then undo the headcollar and rope. Fasten the headcollar round his neck while you brush his face gently with the body brush or a special face brush.

3 Standing to one side of the pony, hold out the tail. Release a few hairs at a time and brush them with the body brush. Undo any knots with your fingers.

Sponging eyes, nose and dock

The corners of a pony's eyes, the nostrils, the muzzle, if it is dirty, and the dock area under the tail should be cleaned every day with damp sponges. Use different sponges for the face and for the dock, and remember which is which!

1 Dampen the sponge, squeeze out the water and wipe the corners of the eyes downwards.

2 Rinse the sponge and use it to clean round the pony's mouth and inside his nostrils.

3 Using a different sponge, clean the dock, including the underside of the tail.

Quartering

Quartering means a quick brushing over of a horse or pony to remove stable stains and shavings, or straw from the mane and tail. This will make him look tidy before going out for exercise. The real work of grooming is done after exercise. In cold weather the rug can be left over the forehand or quarters to keep the pony warm.

Fold back the rug over the pony's quarters while grooming his forehand. Do both sides, then fold the rug forwards over his forehand so you can groom his quarters.

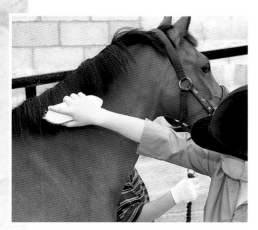

4 To clean the mane and remove any tangles, first brush it out thoroughly with the body brush. For a final neat finish, dampen the water brush and use it to lay the mane in place.

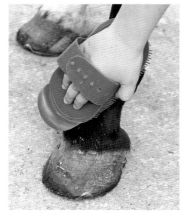

5 Although dried mud should be removed first, you can use a plastic or rubber curry comb instead of a dandy brush to remove any you may have missed on the legs.

6 The final step is to go all over the pony's body with a stable rubber. This is a cotton cloth that removes any remaining traces of dust and loose hairs, and gives a glossy finish to the coat.

Feet and foot care

Taking care of a horse's or pony's feet is one of the most important tasks an owner must carry out. A pony's feet must be sound. You should check and pick out a pony's feet before and after riding, and on non-riding days, do it at least once. You must also have them regularly trimmed by a farrier, and shod (pages 110–111) if you ride on rough tracks and roads.

When feet need attention

If a pony's feet have not been regularly trimmed, the horn of the hoof will grow long and ragged, and may split. When a pony does a lot of road work, the shoes will wear thin quickly and need renewing regularly. Overgrowth of the feet makes the shoe nails work loose, and the shoe may come off.

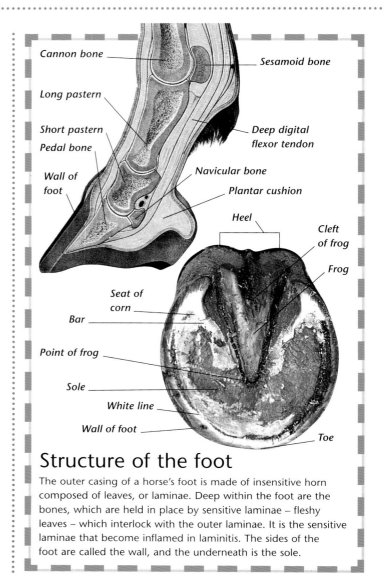

Structure of the foot

The outer casing of a horse's foot is made of insensitive horn composed of leaves, or laminae. Deep within the foot are the bones, which are held in place by sensitive laminae – fleshy leaves – which interlock with the outer laminae. It is the sensitive laminae that become inflamed in laminitis. The sides of the foot are called the wall, and the underneath is the sole.

Overgrown hooves
If the hoof is allowed to become overgrown, the toes get too long and turn up, and the pony's weight goes back on his heels, altering the foot's balance. It can take a long time to correct this.

Raised clenches
When the foot has been neglected and allowed to grow too long, the clenches (the ends of the nails that hold the shoe on) rise out of the hoof wall. The pony can injure himself on them and may lose the shoe.

Stones lodged in the foot

Sometimes horses pick up small stones in their feet, which lodge in the grooves on either side of the frog. If they get wedged in, they can damage the foot, causing pain and lameness. You can remove them by digging them out with a hoof pick.

Picking up and picking out a foot

Be positive in your actions when you pick up a pony's foot. Slide your hand firmly down each leg so you do not tickle him. Always use a hoof pick from the heel of the foot to the toe, paying particular attention to the grooves between the frog and the bars, and to the cleft of the frog itself.

Oiling the feet

Applying hoof oil to a horse's feet makes them look smart, but you should not do it too often or it can prevent the hoof absorbing moisture. Pick out the feet and scrub off any mud with a water brush before you start. Let the feet dry, then apply the oil with a small brush. Hoof oil will not improve the quality of the foot's horn. Only a special diet can do this.

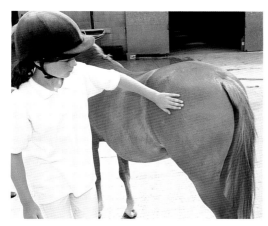

1 When you want to pick up and examine a pony's hind foot, start by putting your hand on the side of his hindquarters and sliding it down towards his leg.

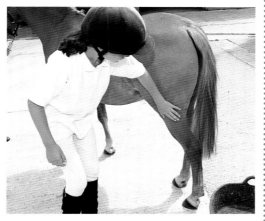

2 Pass your hand firmly down the back of his hind leg. Do not be nervous when you are handling a pony or he will sense it and become nervous as well.

3 Continue down the back of his leg until you reach the hock. Keep your own feet away from the pony's in case he treads on you.

4 When you reach the pony's hock, bring your hand round to the front of his leg and move downwards over the cannon bone.

5 When you reach the fetlock joint, grasp it firmly and try to lift it, saying "Up" as you do so. Crouch – do not kneel – beside the pony.

6 Hold the pony's foot in one hand while you use the hoof pick from the heel towards the toe in the other. A skip is useful for the dirt.

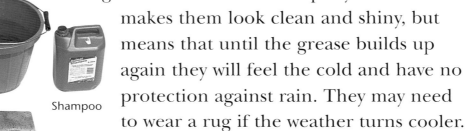

Washing a pony

Only wash a horse or pony if it is absolutely necessary. Choose a warm, sunny and windless day. Washing removes much of the grease from a horse's or pony's coat. This makes them look clean and shiny, but means that until the grease builds up again they will feel the cold and have no protection against rain. They may need to wear a rug if the weather turns cooler.

Bucket of water

Shampoo

Sweat scraper

Sponge

Equipment for washing
Before you start, collect all the necessary equipment and put it where you can reach it easily.

Washing routine

It is important to keep the shampoo out of the pony's eyes, so when you are washing his neck and mane make sure his head is held up. Do not shampoo his face, just wipe it over with a clean, damp sponge.

1 Tie up the pony in the yard where the water can drain away. Fill a bucket with warm water and mix in the shampoo.

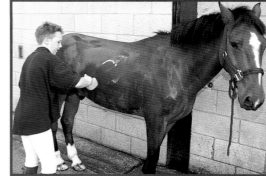

2 Dip the sponge in the water and rub it over the pony's coat in the direction of the hair. Cover the whole body, but not the head.

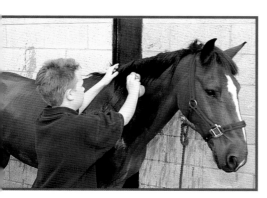

3 Wash the mane with the sponge, then rinse off all traces of the shampoo with another sponge and several buckets of water, or use a hose if the pony does not mind.

4 After rinsing, use the sweat scraper to remove the excess water, pulling it across the pony's body following the lie of the coat. If you do not have a sweat scraper, you can use the side of your hand.

5 Gently comb out the wet mane. If there are knots and tangles in it, undo them carefully with your fingers before combing. Do not try to drag them out with the comb or you will pull out the hairs.

Rinsing the saddle patch

In warm weather, when a horse returns from exercise with a sweaty saddle patch, you can hose him, if this does not scare him, or sponge off the sweat.

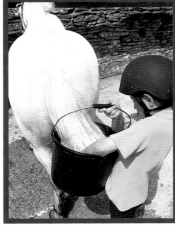

1 Wash the top of the tail with a wet sponge, warm water and shampoo, as you did the pony's body.

2 Rinse the tail in several buckets of clean water, swishing it round with your hand.

Washing a pony's tail

A pony's tail may need washing frequently, especially if it is a pale colour. Doing so will not chill the pony. Use a bucket of warm water and shampoo, lifting up the bucket to get as much of the tail in it as possible. Hold up the bucket with one hand while you squeeze dirt out of the tail with the other.

6 Rub an old towel all over the pony in the direction of the hair to dry him off as much as possible. Squeeze out the water from his mane in the towel and dry his neck underneath it. Do not forget to dry his legs and heels as well.

7 On a hot day the pony will dry naturally in the sun. If the sky clouds over, put an anti-sweat sheet or a cooler rug over him, and walk him up and down round the yard until he is dry, to prevent him from catching a chill.

Clipping a pony

Horses and ponies grow thick coats in winter. If they are worked hard they sweat a lot and lose condition. To avoid this, the areas where they sweat the most have the hair clipped off. A clipped horse or pony needs rugging to keep it warm when it is not working, even if it lives in a stable. Clippers must be handled with care, and the job is best done by an adult.

The hair is completely clipped off from the horse's head and neck.

Bandit clip
The horse is clipped all over except for his face, where the hair is left as protection from the rain. It is also a useful clip for a head-shy horse.

A bib clip runs in a straight line down the side of the neck.

Hunter clip
All the hair is clipped except for the saddle patch and the legs, which are left unclipped for protection against sores and thorns.

Bib clip
The pony is clipped on the face, and the front of the neck, chest and shoulders. This clip is used for a horse or pony that sweats a lot on the neck.

Belly clip
The hair is removed from the belly and up between the forelegs. A variation is to clip the hair on the underside of the neck, too.

Different types of clip

The different styles of clip reflect the amount of work a horse or pony is expected to do. Some hard-working horses are fully clipped; others have areas of winter coat left on for protection against the weather, saddle sores, cuts and thorns.

Trace clip
This is a popular clip for working ponies. Hair is removed from the underside of the neck, the belly and the lower part of the body.

Clipping equipment

Clipping machines are usually electrically operated. They have a number of blades, from fine to coarse, depending on the type of hair to be cut. The blades need oiling and cleaning regularly when in use.

Main clippers

Small clippers

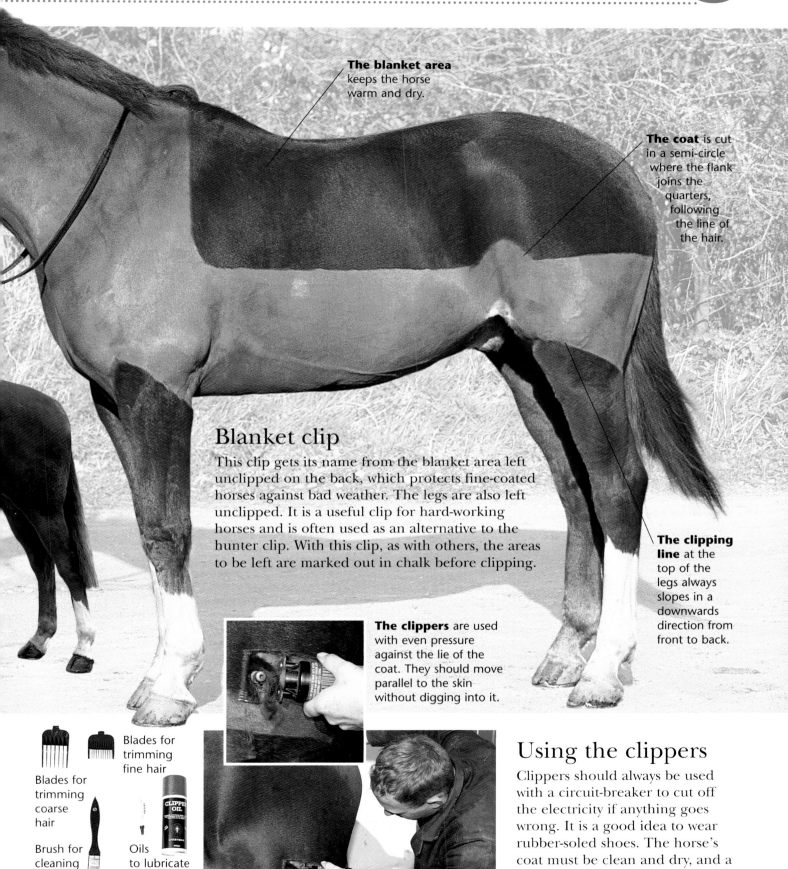

The blanket area keeps the horse warm and dry.

The coat is cut in a semi-circle where the flank joins the quarters, following the line of the hair.

Blanket clip

This clip gets its name from the blanket area left unclipped on the back, which protects fine-coated horses against bad weather. The legs are also left unclipped. It is a useful clip for hard-working horses and is often used as an alternative to the hunter clip. With this clip, as with others, the areas to be left are marked out in chalk before clipping.

The clipping line at the top of the legs always slopes in a downwards direction from front to back.

The clippers are used with even pressure against the lie of the coat. They should move parallel to the skin without digging into it.

Blades for trimming fine hair

Blades for trimming coarse hair

Brush for cleaning clippers

Oils to lubricate clippers

Using the clippers

Clippers should always be used with a circuit-breaker to cut off the electricity if anything goes wrong. It is a good idea to wear rubber-soled shoes. The horse's coat must be clean and dry, and a haynet may help keep him quiet.

Choosing a rug

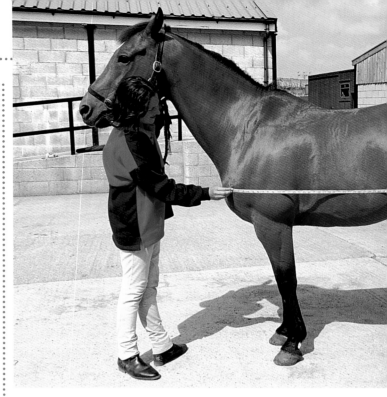

When a horse or pony has been clipped, he needs to wear a rug to make up for the loss of his winter coat and to keep him warm. On cold winter nights, he may need more than one rug, or an extra blanket under the rug. To be comfortable, the rug should be deep enough to cover the belly and should reach down to the root of the tail. Clipped horses are turned out in New Zealand rugs to keep off the rain.

Measuring for a rug

You need a long tape measure and an assistant to do this. Take the measurement from the centre of the horse's chest to the furthest point of his hindquarters. Rug sizes go up in about 7–8cm increases, so you have to buy the nearest size.

Types of rug

Rugs are made in a bewildering variety of styles, shapes and materials. The latter may be natural, such as cotton, wool or jute; or synthetic, usually nylon or polyester. All rugs fasten across the front of the chest with either one or two straps. They are then held in place either by a roller, which goes across the horse's back and round his belly like a girth, or by crossed surcingles. These are sewn on to the right-hand side of the rug, and pass under the horse's belly to fasten on the left side, crossing over from front to back as they do so. There are special kinds of rugs for specific purposes, though most horses and ponies just need a stable rug and a New Zealand rug.

An anti-sweat sheet is a mesh rug used on a sweating horse to prevent chills as he cools down.

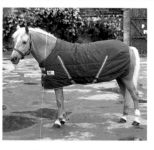

A stable rug keeps the horse warm indoors. It may be quilted or made of jute.

A New Zealand rug is waterproof and is used when the horse is out in the field in winter.

A summer sheet is a cotton rug used to keep the horse clean at shows and when travelling.

An exercise sheet is used to keep the horse's back warm during winter exercise.

A hooded New Zealand rug also keeps the pony's neck warm in bad winter weather.

How to put on a rug

When you put on a pony's rug, do not fling it on to his back, lower it gently. Put on the rug well forwards of where it should lie so you can slide it back into place, thus leaving the pony's coat lying flat.

Crossed surcingles

These should be adjusted by sliding the buckles so they fit comfortably round the pony's belly. They do not need to be tight – there should be room for your hand to fit between them and the pony.

1 Tie up the pony. Carry the rug to him folded in half, with the back part folded forwards over the front part.

2 Holding the rug in both hands, lower it carefully on to the pony's back in front of where it should fit.

3 Unfold the back part of the rug and lay it over the pony's quarters. As you do so, check that it is lying straight.

4 Fasten the breast straps, then slide the rug back until it lies in the correct position on the pony's back.

5 Undo the surcingles on the right side. Reach under the pony's belly for them from the left and fasten them.

6 Finally, make sure that the rug does not press down on the pony's withers and that it is not too tight across his chest.

Roller

A rug may be secured by a roller, which fits quite tightly round the horse. An anti-cast roller has an arch in the centre to prevent a horse from getting stuck, or cast, when he rolls.

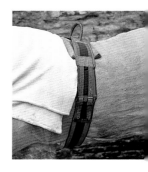

Anti-cast roller

Leg straps

New Zealand rugs are held in place by leg straps, one of which is looped through the other to prevent them rubbing. They must be fitted correctly.

How to take off a rug

Tie up the pony. If the rug has a roller, undo it first and lift it off the pony's back. Make sure that the breast straps, surcingles and any leg straps are unfastened before removing the rug.

1 When you have undone the surcingles, tie them loosely in place on the right-hand side.

2 Undo the breast straps. Fold back the front of the rug to lie over the back.

3 Holding the folded rug with both hands, slide it backwards off the pony's quarters.

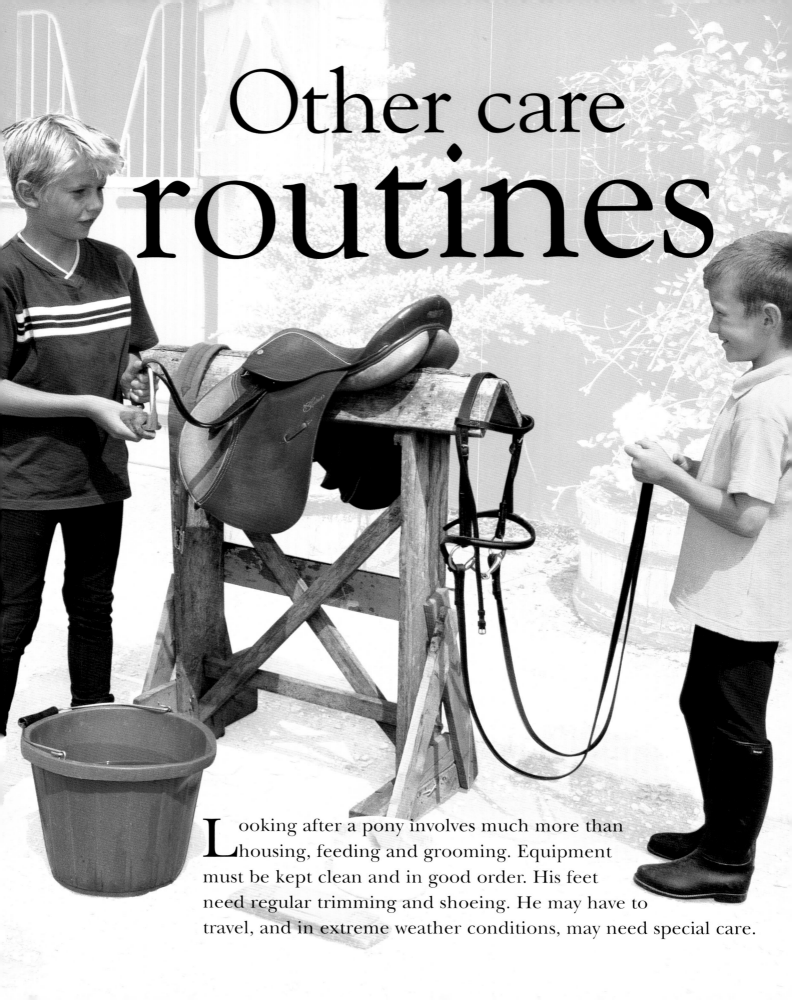

Other care
routines

Looking after a pony involves much more than housing, feeding and grooming. Equipment must be kept clean and in good order. His feet need regular trimming and shoeing. He may have to travel, and in extreme weather conditions, may need special care.

Checking the legs
When you get back to the stable, check the pony's legs for small cuts or any thorns he may have picked up, and feel for any heat or swelling.

Walking home
Provided you are not on a busy road, loosen the girth by one hole and let your pony walk on a loose rein to stretch his neck muscles.

At the end of a ride

Horses and ponies can get hot, sweaty and excitable during a ride. Always walk your pony the last kilometre or two home to let him cool off and calm down. At the end of a hard day, dismount, run the stirrups up, loosen the girth and lead him home.

Care after exercise

O n your return home, unsaddle the pony, check him over and pick out his feet. Brush off any mud or sweat marks. In hot weather, you can sponge these off. Put on his rug, or an anti-sweat sheet, and if he is tired and thirsty, offer him half a bucket of tepid water. You can give him more later. Give a stabled pony a haynet before his feed. If he lives out, and is not cold or sweating, you can turn him out.

Rubbing the ears
A tired, wet horse may have cold ears. You can restore the circulation to the ears by grasping them at the base and pulling them gently through your closed hands.

All rugged up
If the pony is dry, brush off any mud before putting on his rug. If he is wet, thatch him by putting straw under the rug. Bandage wet and muddy legs over straw or gamgee.

Shoeing a pony

Ponies' and horses' feet grow like your fingernails, and need trimming every six to eight weeks to keep them in good condition. Shoeing prevents the feet from wearing down too quickly when the pony is exercised on hard surfaces like roads. The person who trims and shoes a pony is called a farrier. Most farriers have mobile forges and travel round to work at their clients' premises.

Hot shoeing

When a shoe is heated in a furnace before being tried on a pony's foot the process is called hot shoeing. Because the horn of the foot is insensitive, like your nails, the pony cannot feel it. A pony may need new shoes each time the farrier visits, but if the shoes are not very worn, the farrier will simply reshape them and use them again.

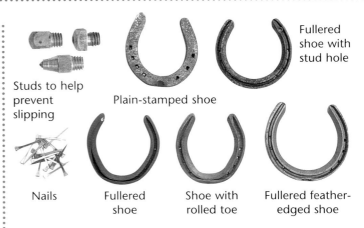

Studs to help prevent slipping

Plain-stamped shoe

Fullered shoe with stud hole

Nails

Fullered shoe

Shoe with rolled toe

Fullered feather-edged shoe

Types of shoe

Most horses and ponies wear fullered shoes, which have a groove running round them to give a better grip in the mud. Farriers can make special types of shoes to correct most horses' and ponies' foot problems, as well as shoes for various kinds of work.

1 Using the buffer and mallet, the farrier cuts the nail ends, or clenches, that hold the shoe on to the foot.

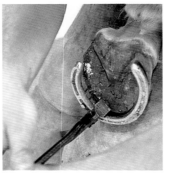

2 When he has cut the clenches, he levers off the shoe with pincers, starting at the heel and moving towards the toe.

3 He neatly cuts away the excess growth of the horn all the way round the foot using the hoof cutters.

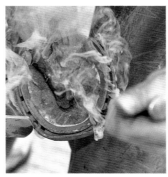

8 He then tries the shoe in place on the hoof. The heat burns the horn, causing it to smoke.

9 When he is satisfied, he cools the shoe in a bucket of water before starting to nail it on to the pony's foot.

10 He hammers the nails through holes in the shoe to hold it in place, starting at the toe and working back.

Fitting studs

So that horses and ponies can be ridden across country in wet or muddy conditions, studs are sometimes screwed into special holes in the heels of their shoes.

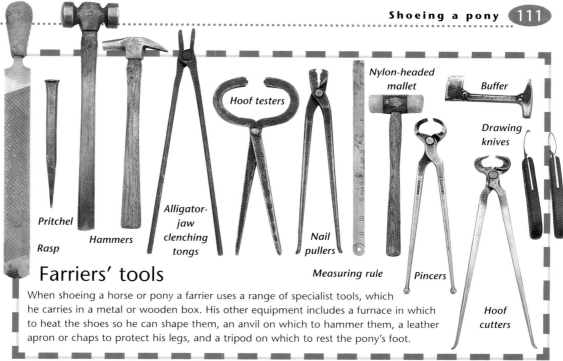

Pritchel

Rasp

Hammers

Alligator-jaw clenching tongs

Hoof testers

Nail pullers

Measuring rule

Nylon-headed mallet

Buffer

Drawing knives

Pincers

Hoof cutters

Farriers' tools

When shoeing a horse or pony a farrier uses a range of specialist tools, which he carries in a metal or wooden box. His other equipment includes a furnace in which to heat the shoes so he can shape them, an anvil on which to hammer them, a leather apron or chaps to protect his legs, and a tripod on which to rest the pony's foot.

4 He tidies up the wall of the foot, the sole and frog, cutting off any ragged bits with a drawing knife.

5 Using the rasp, he makes sure that the weight-bearing surface of the foot is absolutely smooth and level.

6 He then heats the shoe in an oven called a furnace until it is red-hot, handling it carefully with pincers.

7 He hammers the hot shoe into shape on the anvil, still holding it with the pincers and reheating it if necessary.

11 The nails come out of the side of the hoof and the farrier twists off their ends with the claw of a hammer.

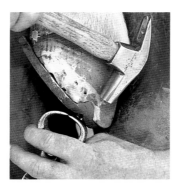

12 Resting the shoe on the pincers, he hammers down the projecting nail ends to form the clenches.

13 With the foot on a tripod, he uses the rasp to smooth the ends of the clenches and the rim of the hoof wall.

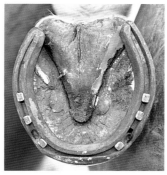

14 The finished foot should look neat and even, with six or more nails holding the new shoe in place.

Travelling safely

I f you wish to take part in riding club events, shows or gymkhanas you will need to transport your pony in a horsebox or a trailer. Once they get used to it, most horses and ponies do not mind this, and learn to brace themselves against the movement of the vehicle. In doing so, however, they may knock their legs, so they need to wear protective clothing. They also wear rugs to keep them warm and clean.

Storage
Water can be carried in a large plastic container.

Providing food and water

While travelling, a haynet will keep your pony happy. Store hay for your return inside the box rather than hanging it outside where it may be contaminated by exhaust fumes. On a long journey, you may also need to take water.

Travel boots
Shaped and padded travel boots fit round the lower part of the pony's legs and are held in place by several Velcro straps.

Boots and bandages

To protect a horse's or pony's legs you can either use special travel boots or bandages. Travel boots cover the legs from the knee or hock to the coronet at the top of the hoof (pages 14–15). If bandages are used, the horse or pony may also need to wear kneecaps and hock boots to cover his joints.

Travel bandages
Used over felt padding, these are put on in the same way as first-aid bandages (see pages 120–121).

1 Start by laying the bandage across the top of the pony's tail, leaving the end sticking up.

2 Then take the bandage under the tail and bring it round to the top, holding the end.

3 After a couple of turns of bandage round the tail, fold down the end you left out.

Bandaging a pony's tail

The top part of a pony's tail is bandaged before travelling to stop him rubbing it against the back of the box. Bandaging also lays the hairs flat and keeps the tail tidy. The bandage needs to fit quite firmly. To prevent it becoming soiled, the bandaged tail can then be folded up and secured with an elastic band.

Travel essentials

Your pony's tack, plus saddle soap, sponges, etc., to give it a final clean

Your riding clothes if you are going to a show

Food and water – for both you and your pony!

Any documents you may need – tickets, entry forms, etc.

First-aid kit for you both

Loading your pony

Most ponies will walk up the ramp of a horsebox or trailer quite happily, but if yours is unhappy about it, let him take his time. If he still hesitates, ask a helper to put one of his front feet on the ramp. He will then usually walk in without a problem. Food may help.

Walk confidently up the ramp.

Don't pull your pony.

Reward him when he goes in.

Ready to go

A single pony in a double trailer travels better on the side nearer the centre of the road. Tie him up quite short, and put the bar or breeching strap across. You can use the other compartment for luggage.

Unloading your pony

Untie the pony, leaving his rope through the ring so he thinks he is still tied up. If your trailer has a front ramp, put it down, then remove the bar or strap. Lead him down the ramp slowly. To unload backwards, ask a helper to stand at the side to keep the pony moving straight back.

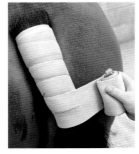

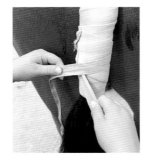

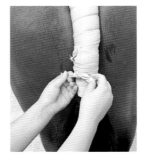

4 Wrap the bandage over the folded-down end to prevent it from slipping.

5 Continue bandaging down the tail until you reach the end of the dock.

6 Cross the strings, take them round to the back and cross them again.

7 Tie the strings round the bandage in a neat bow to hold it securely in place.

8 Fold a layer of bandage over the bow to stop it from coming undone.

Removing a tail bandage

To remove the tail bandage, unfold the part over the bow, untie the strings and slide the whole thing off in one movement, laying the hair flat and smooth as you do so. Roll up the bandage from the strings end with the strings folded inside.

Summer and winter care

Extremes of temperature and weather may mean that a horse or pony requires special care. In hot summer weather, horses seek shade, and an escape from the flies that can make their lives miserable. In the depths of winter, a field-kept pony will have little to eat, and the ground may be muddy or frozen. The water supply may freeze up, too. We have to solve all these problems.

Preventing sunburn

Horses and ponies that have pink noses can suffer from sunburn. It particularly affects stabled animals, who may stand with their heads over the stable door for hours in the sun. You can protect them from sunburn by applying a sunblock cream made for use on human skin.

Fly fringe
A fly fringe can be fitted over a headcollar, or worn on its own. As the horse moves, the strings keep flies out of his eyes.

Fly repellent
A number of products are available to help ward off flies. Most are poured on to a cloth and wiped on the pony's coat. Some ponies do not mind spray products.

Coping with fly nuisance

Horses and ponies that suffer greatly from flies are best stabled in the daytime and turned out at night. If this is not possible, then fly fringes, or netting veils, which cover most of the face, can help. Horses provide their own protection by standing in pairs nose to tail, each swishing the flies off the other's face.

Leg and foot care

In winter, a horse's or pony's legs and feet need special attention. Constant exposure to wet and mud can cause mud fever (page 123), so it is worth trying to protect them from this. Riding on ice is dangerous because your pony may fall, but you can ride in snow if you grease his feet.

Foot greasing
Putting grease in the foot stops snow from packing inside it.

Leg greasing
Applying Vaseline or liquid paraffin to a horse's lower legs and heels helps keep the mud and wet off them.

Keeping warm
A clipped horse or pony will stay warm in the coldest weather if he has sufficient food and if he wears a thick enough rug. It is better to add an under-blanket or another rug for warmth than to shut the top half of his stable door.

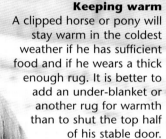

Breaking the ice
In severe weather, the water in field troughs and even in stable buckets will freeze. To ensure that your pony has enough to drink, you must break the ice several times a day. If possible, use warm water for topping up because this will refreeze less quickly.

Essential winter care

Native ponies can live out without rugs all winter if they have enough to eat. Depending on the weather, the pasture, the pony and his work, he will need some hay and possibly hard feed from mid-winter to spring.

Health
care

Horses, and especially ponies, are hardy animals. Provided you follow a few simple rules, they stay healthy. However, things can go wrong, so you need to know how to cope when they do.

Pricked ears
Although ears laid back are a sign of bad temper rather than ill health, pricked ears show that the pony is interested in what is happening. His ears move to catch the slightest sound.

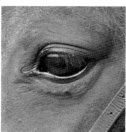

Bright eyes
A pony's eyes should be bright and clear. The pupils should dilate in the dark and contract in bright light. The eyes should not run, though a small amount of dirt may collect in the corners.

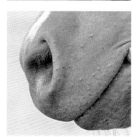

Dry nose
A horse's nose should be dry. Some animals that are allergic to dust may have a slight, watery nasal discharge. But thick mucus, especially if greenish or yellow, is a sign of infection.

Other things to check

A healthy horse or pony should be neither fat nor thin. Sticking-out ribs and a pot belly are signs of worms, as is a cough. The horse's breathing should be relaxed and regular – noisy breathing may be a sign of lung disease or dust allergies. At rest, the horse should feel warm, with cool feet and legs. His droppings should be formed and should just break on reaching the ground.

Signs of good health

A healthy pony has bright eyes, a shiny coat, a keen appetite, and is interested in everything that goes on around him. Ponies are inquisitive, and will come and investigate what you are doing. Out in a field, they stay together in a group. A pony that keeps away from the others may not be well.

Signs of ill health

If a pony stands with his head down looking unhappy, if his eyes are dull and his coat is in poor condition, he may be ill. Pinch his skin between your finger and thumb. It should spring straight back into place. If it does not, the pony may be dehydrated (lacking water).

Full of life

Although horses and ponies in a field spend most of the time grazing, they will play and gallop around, especially if they are young. This helps them get exercise and also keeps them fit. They only sleep for about four hours a day, and one always stands guard while the others lie down. Horses and ponies can also doze standing up.

Health routine

Regular worming and vaccination are essential to help keep a horse or pony in good health. It is important to know your pony's usual pulse, temperature and respiration (breathing) rates, and also to be able to recognize its normal behaviour. Being aware of these things will help you to spot anything that is wrong and remedy it very quickly.

The vet watches the pony move. If he drags a hind toe, this may indicate lameness in that leg.

Checking the pulse and respiration

Feel for the pulse with your fingers just under the pony's jawbone. Count the number of beats you feel in one minute. It should be 35 to 45 when the pony is resting. The pony's respiration rate is 10 to 20 breaths a minute at rest.

Checking legs

A pony's legs should feel cool and be free from swellings. By running your hand down each leg in turn every day, you will be able to feel any swellings or heat, which may indicate an injury even if the pony does not seem lame.

Trotting in hand is the easiest way to check for lameness.

Lameness

If you walk or trot a horse or pony on hard ground, such as a yard, it is possible for someone watching to tell on which leg he is lame. With foreleg lameness, a pony will nod his head as the sound front leg hits the ground.

Keep a firm hold of the thermometer for two minutes before you withdraw and read it. Make sure you do not let go!

Taking the temperature

If you think your pony may be ill, ask an adult to help you take his temperature. The normal temperature for a horse or pony is between 37.5°C and 38.5°C. Grease the bulb of the thermometer and insert it gently into the pony's anus.

Worming

Horses and ponies need worming every four to eight weeks. The wormer may be a powder, which you sprinkle in your pony's food, or a paste, which is squirted on to his tongue with an applicator. Ponies don't seem to mind the taste. You should ask an adult to help you worm your pony.

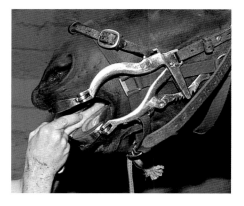

Care of the teeth

Horses' and ponies' back teeth often wear unevenly, making the mouth uncomfortable. It is a good idea to have them checked each year by a vet or an equine dentist. He or she will rasp smooth any sharp edges, using a gag to keep the pony's mouth open and avoid being bitten.

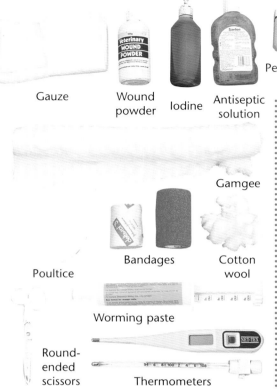

Gauze

Wound powder

Iodine

Antiseptic solution

Petroleum jelly

Gamgee

Poultice

Bandages

Cotton wool

Worming paste

Round-ended scissors

Thermometers

First aid

It is useful to know how to carry out basic first-aid routines to help you deal with a horse's or pony's minor injuries and problems yourself. But if a pony shows obvious signs of illness, or is lame or badly injured, you should ask the advice of a knowledgeable adult, as it may be necessary to call out the vet. Prompt veterinary attention can prevent a problem from getting worse.

First-aid kit

It is a good idea to have a first-aid kit handy. Keep it in a clean, dry place and check it from time to time. If you use any of the contents, replace them so they will be there the next time you need to use them in an emergency.

Preventing infection

Make sure you use clean cotton wool.

Clean the wound from the centre out.

Thorough cleaning of a wound will prevent infection and help it to heal quickly. Clip off the surrounding hair. Pour warm water into a clean container and add some antiseptic. Dip clean cotton wool into the solution, squeeze it out, and use it to clean the wound. Use more cotton wool until the wound is clean. If the wound bleeds a lot, or is near a joint or tendon, call out the vet.

Hosing the legs

Hosing an injured leg with cold water can reduce swelling and pain. Ask a helper to hold the pony and just trickle the hose on his leg to start with. Then hose the leg for about 15 minutes, stop, let it warm up again, and then repeat the procedure once or twice more.

Leg bandages

Bandages may be used to hold a dressing in place, to support injured or swollen legs and to keep cold, wet legs warm. Bandages are put over a layer of padding called gamgee. When bandaging the legs, crouch – do not kneel – beside the pony.

Applying wound powder

You can treat minor cuts and scratches with antiseptic wound powder, which you puff on to the wound after cleaning it. As well as helping to prevent the entry of infection, wound powder helps to keep flies away.

1 Bandage any dressing in place, then wrap gamgee round the leg. Cover the coronet and make sure the gamgee is kept flat.

2 Start applying the bandage just below the knee or hock. Hold the end in place until you have secured it with a few more turns.

1 Cut the poultice to the size you need and soak it in either hot or cold water. Squeeze out the water while keeping the poultice flat.

2 Place the poultice over the sole of the pony's foot and start to bandage it in place. It is easiest to use a stretch, self-adhesive bandage.

3 Bandage in a figure-of-eight shape round the hoof. When you have finished, tape thick cotton wool or a bag round the foot.

Finished poultice bandage

Tubbing a foot

Tubbing means putting a horse's foot and lower leg in a bucket of warm water containing Epsom salts. This is used to help draw out infections of the hoof. The horse needs to stand with his leg in the bucket for 10 to 15 minutes, preferably twice a day. Unless you know the horse is quiet, ask an adult to help.

Applying a foot poultice

Poultices may be used hot or cold. A hot poultice is used to draw out infection from a wound or abscess, a cold one to reduce swelling, for example, when the foot is bruised. You can buy chemically prepared poultices, made of cotton wool and gauze.

3 Work down the leg and over the fetlock and pastern until you reach the top of the hoof. Try to keep the tension even as you work.

4 When you reach the coronet, apply the bandage in the opposite direction and work your way back up the pony's leg.

5 By the time you have got to the end of the bandage, you should have arrived back at the place on the leg where you began.

6 Secure the bandage with Velcro straps or tapes. Tie the tapes neatly on the inside or the outside of the pony's leg.

7 The finished bandage should be firm but not too tight. You should be able to see a layer of gamgee at its top and bottom.

Common ailments

E ven the best cared-for horse or pony will occasionally suffer from a minor ailment. Once you can recognize what is wrong, you can carry out simple treatment. Look out for signs of abnormal behaviour in your pony, for areas of sore, rubbed skin, for lumps and swellings, and for any signs of lameness. Laminitis and colic are the most serious problems you are likely to encounter. Both can be caused by a pony over-eating.

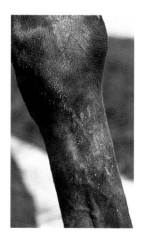

Bot-fly eggs

Little yellow specks on a pony's lower legs in summer are bot-fly eggs. Ask an adult to scrape them off with a knife. If the pony licks the eggs, bot larvae develop in his mouth and stomach. Worming with ivermectin in early winter destroys the bot-fly larvae.

Rubbing mane

Even if they do not have sweet itch, many horses and ponies rub their manes and tails in summer, which looks unsightly and causes soreness. Rub in benzyl benzoate, or protect the horse with a special lightweight hooded rug and a fly screen for the face.

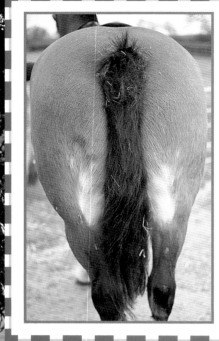

Sweet itch

Sweet itch is the name of an allergy to the bite of tiny midges, which causes some ponies to rub themselves raw to try and get rid of the irritation. The mane and tail are usually affected.

The midges mostly bite early in the morning and at dusk, so the best way to avoid sweet itch with a susceptible pony is to stable him at these times.

Benzyl benzoate, from the chemist, rubbed into the roots of the mane and tail, helps relieve the symptoms of sweet itch.

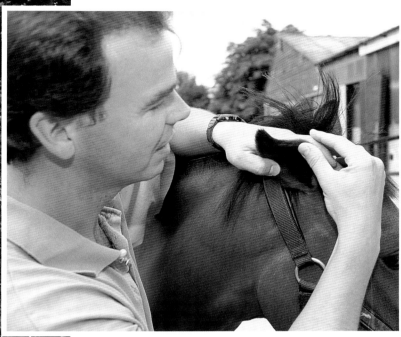

Ear plaques
Areas of white skin in the ears, called plaques, are harmless and do not need treatment.

Looking for mites
You may not see the mites, which are tiny, but thick brown wax in the ears gives them away.

Problems with a pony's ears

Shaking of the head, rubbing of the ears and a discharge from the ears are all signs of ear problems. The symptoms may simply be the result of ear mites (tiny parasites), but they could also indicate an infection. If you suspect something is wrong with a pony's ears, have them examined by a vet.

Symptoms of colic

Colic is a common digestive problem, and can be very serious. Affected ponies often roll, but then do not shake themselves afterwards. They may lie down and get up again frequently. If badly affected, they will sweat and be in obvious pain. If you see signs of colic, call out the vet immediately.

Swollen leg
This swelling on the lower leg might be the result of a knock or a sprain. Hosing the leg (page 120) may help.

Swellings in the legs

Swellings can be caused by ligament or tendon injuries; bruising; splints, which are bony enlargements; arthritis and other conditions. They may feel hard or soft, there may be heat in the leg, and the pony may be lame. It is generally best to seek veterinary advice.

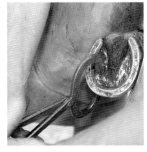

Mud fever
Sore, cracked heels need treatment by a vet.

Hoof testers
Check for laminitis by applying pressure.

Mud fever and laminitis

Mud fever is a winter problem; ponies that eat too much rich summer grass can get laminitis, a very painful inflammation of the hoof. It usually affects the front feet, which feel hot, and the pony may be lame. If a pony has symptoms of laminitis, get him in from the field and call the vet.

Caring for a sick pony

A sick or injured pony that is confined to a stable likes to follow his normal routine as far as possible. Provided he is not too ill, you can give him a light daily grooming. Keep him warm with rugs if necessary, and make sure he always has clean water to drink. If he cannot go out at all, pick him a few handfuls of grass to enjoy each day, as long as the vet allows it. Never feed a pony lawn trimmings.

Giving a pony medicine

Medicines come in different forms – powders, pills and liquids. Powders and liquids can be mixed in the feed. Putting them in a tasty, moist food, such as soaked sugar beet, helps to disguise the taste. Pills can be crushed between two spoons and fed in the same way. Liquids may also be dropped on to the horse's tongue or inside the lower lip, or squirted into the mouth with a syringe.

Hide a pill or capsule in a slice of apple. Cut a slit in the apple and push the pill down into it so the pulp of the fruit surrounds the pill and masks the taste.

Powdered medicine can be sprinkled on to a slice of bread with treacle. Fold the bread to hide the powder and tear or cut it into bite-sized pieces.

Convalescence

A horse or pony confined to a stable for a long time gets very bored, especially when he is feeling better. Divide his hay ration into several smaller nets to keep him occupied. Visit him frequently, and bring him titbits. Some horses and ponies like a radio left on for company.

Things to play with

If the horse or pony is allowed to move around, he may enjoy playing with a horse football. You can buy several types of horse toys, which are designed to be safe, and impossible for the horse to puncture if he bites or kicks them.

Stable toys include hanging balls, on which you can smear treacle.

Feline friend

When a horse or pony has to be confined to the stable for long periods and he has no other equine friends around, he may appreciate the company of a friendly household cat or dog, especially if you cannot visit him as often as you would like.

Grazing on the lawn

If your pony cannot go out into the field but is allowed out of his stable, spare a few minutes each day to give him some in-hand grazing, provided the vet allows it. It is also a good way of keeping the lawn trimmed!

The road to recovery

Once the pony has recovered from his illness, you must get him fit before he can resume normal work. Start by giving him gentle exercise. A good way to do this is with a few minutes' in-hand walking each day, gradually increasing the time and distance. If you are leading him on a road, keep him well into the side, and walk in the direction of the traffic. Position yourself between the pony and the traffic.

Wear a hard hat and gloves when leading a pony on the road.

A pony should wear a bridle when being led on the road.

Wear light-coloured or reflective clothing

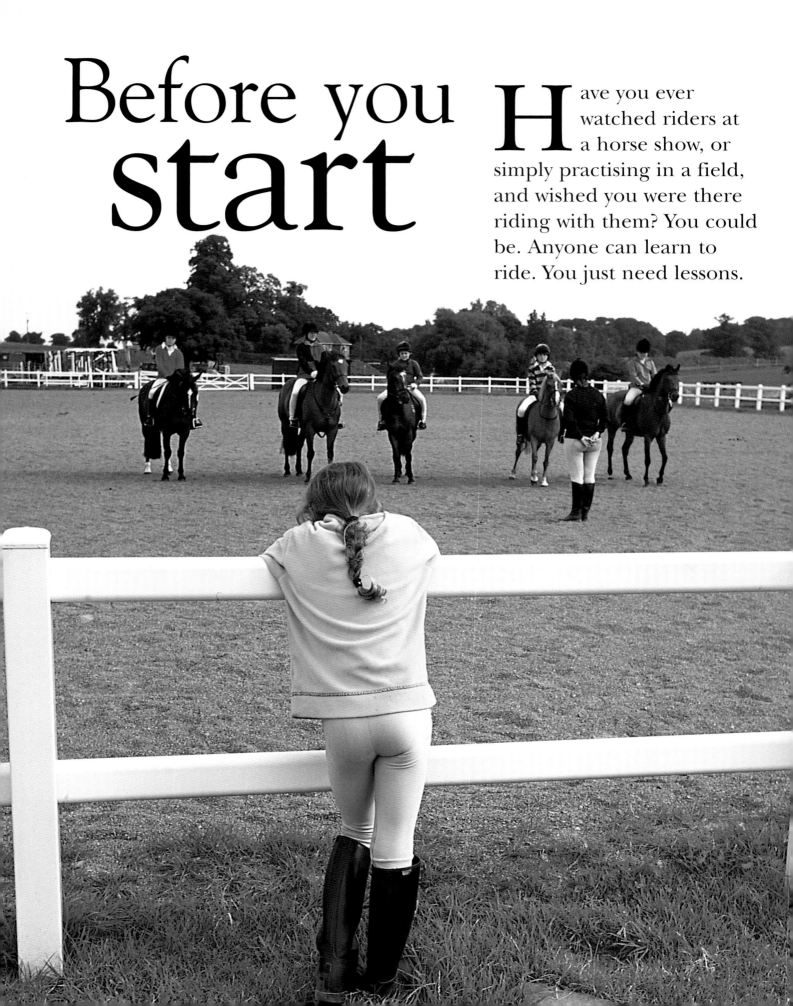

Before you start

Have you ever watched riders at a horse show, or simply practising in a field, and wished you were there riding with them? You could be. Anyone can learn to ride. You just need lessons.

Why have riding lessons?

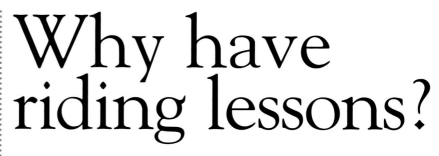

Y ou may be told that, given a quiet pony to practise on, you can learn to ride on your own. Up to a point, this is true. You may learn how to make the pony move forwards, turn and stop. But compare these simple efforts with the style of a top dressage rider, or with the boldness of an eventer, galloping across country. Whether this is your dream, or whether you just want to ride for fun, taking proper lessons will be your first step on the road to success as a rider.

Taking part in events

You may wish to take part in events – in showing, dressage, hunter trials or gymkhanas. If you ride well enough, you may not need to own a pony to compete. You might be able to borrow one, or even be asked to ride for someone else.

Hacking out with friends

Going for a hack in the countryside with your friends is one of the most enjoyable riding activities. You can explore new places, and you may spot all kinds of interesting wildlife, because animals are not afraid of horses. Your ponies, too, will enjoy being ridden out in the company of others.

Riding holidays

A riding holiday may mean pony trekking in Scotland, riding the range like a cowboy in the USA, exploring the mountains of Spain or having intensive lessons with a professional. You will have a wonderful time on a riding holiday, and you will enjoy it all the more if you are a good rider.

Where to have riding lessons

It is important to choose a good riding school when you decide to have lessons. Look for those that are approved by an equestrian organization. Try to visit several schools, and check what facilities they provide. They should be orderly, and have a calm atmosphere.

Friendly instructors

The instructors at a good riding school will be friendly and helpful, even if they may sometimes be quite firm with you! You should be able to ask them questions and, if necessary, talk over with them any difficulties you may have. When they are taking classes, the instructors will wear boots and riding hats. They should also wear gloves when they are leading a horse or pony.

Happy horses

A row of clean, shiny heads looking out over their loose box doors, taking an interest in everything going on, is a good sign. The ponies must look well fed and their stables should be clean. The yard on to which they look out should be swept and tidy.

Tidy tack room

Tack must be clean and well cared for. There should be no cracked leather, fraying girths or stitching coming undone. Tack should be stored in a tidy tack room, which is heated in winter, with the saddles and bridles kept on brackets and hooks.

Lessons in the outdoor school

The riding school will probably have an outdoor school in which lessons are given. This is a fenced arena that may have a surface of bark or sand, kept raked smooth and level. Even if the school is just a fenced-off corner of a field, it should not be deep in mud.

Riding surface
The surface of an indoor school – sand, bark or synthetic granules – stays dry whatever the weather. It must be raked smooth.

The indoor school

An indoor school, usually housed in a large barn, is a great asset to a riding school. Whatever the weather, you can keep dry for your lessons. And, in the winter months, it means you can ride in the late afternoons and evenings, when it is too dark to ride outside.

Watching lessons
Many indoor schools have an area where people can sit or stand to watch lessons in progress. If the indoor school is large enough, the riding school may hold competitions in it during the winter.

When work is over

In summer, at the end of a long day's lessons, the ponies may be turned out into the field to enjoy some well-earned freedom. In winter, they are likely to be stabled at night, and given feed and hay.

Clothes to wear for riding

Headgear
You must always wear a hard hat when riding. You should also wear it when you are leading or lungeing a horse or pony. Whether you choose a traditional hunting cap or a skull cap, you must make sure it is the right size. It should be fitted with a safety harness and comply with the latest safety standards.

A hunting cap has a rigid brim and is covered with fine velvet.

Every sport has its correct clothing, and for riding this means a shirt and tie, a jacket, jodhpurs, boots, hat and gloves. Usually, the dress is more casual. The one essential item of clothing, on all occasions, is a hard hat.

Why wear riding gear?

Jodhpurs and boots are much more comfortable to wear for riding than jeans and shoes. Jodhpurs stop your legs being rubbed against the saddle; boots protect you from knocks from the stirrups.

Casual clothes
For riding lessons, or going out on a hack, you will be comfortable in jodhpurs, boots, gloves, hat, and a shirt worn with a jumper or a jacket if the weather is cool.

Adjustable shoulder strap

Body protector
For any riding activity that involves jumping you should wear a body protector. It is a rigid waistcoat that protects your back in case you fall off.

Riding gloves with palm grips

Gloves

Riding gloves have special surfaces on their palms to help grip the reins. They may have leather or suede palms, or raised rubber pimples, which are useful in wet weather, when reins become very slippery. You should always wear gloves when you are riding, leading or lungeing horses and ponies.

A skull cap is a round, brimless helmet that is usually worn covered by a silk.

Safety harness

Silks with small brims are available in various colours to wear over skull caps.

Adjust the safety harness so that it is comfortable but holds the hat in place.

Skull cap and silk

Shirt and tie

Wool hacking jacket

Body-warmer under jacket

Show gear
To compete in a show or other event you should wear formal riding clothes. You may wear a hacking jacket, or a black or navy show jacket.

Winter wear
A quilted, waterproof jacket is ideal for cold days, and half chaps help keep your legs warm. In wet weather a full-length mac will keep you dry.

Western gear

Traditional Western riding gear means jeans, full-length chaps, fancy boots, a bandanna round the neck, a fringed jacket and a stetson. Many riders dress more casually. To protect their heads, today's young riders all wear hard hats.

Boots

There are two kinds of boots for riding: ankle-length leather jodhpur boots with elasticated sides, and full-length riding boots, which may be made of leather or a synthetic material. Long boots and half chaps, which you can wear with jodhpur boots, protect the inner sides of your legs from being pinched by the stirrup leathers. You can wear shoes when you are riding, but they must be strong and have a smooth, non-ridged sole and a heel.

Jodhpur boots protect your ankles.

Riding boots reach almost up to your knees and fit tightly.

Leather half chaps may fasten with straps or zips.

Measuring a pony

Traditionally, horses and ponies are measured in hands. One hand is equal to about 10cm, which is roughly the width of an adult's hand. Today, ponies are also measured in centimetres.

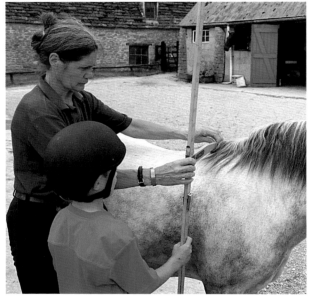

A measuring stick
An upright pole with a sliding bar enables you to read off the pony's height.

On the withers
The horizontal sliding bar rests on the highest point of the pony's withers.

Types of pony

Ponies may be a variety of shapes and sizes. They can be stocky and broad, so your legs can hardly reach round them, or they may be tall and narrow. They can be very hard work to keep moving, or go like the wind. For your first lessons you need a quiet pony. As your riding improves, you may graduate to a more lively one.

The right-sized pony

It is important that the pony you ride is the right size for you. If the pony is too large or too small, you will be unable to use your legs properly to give the correct aids, and you may find it more difficult to balance. If you are too large for the pony, you may also be too heavy for him to carry, and you could injure his back.

Too small a pony
This pony is too small for her rider. The rider's legs are too long to make proper contact with the pony's sides, and she may also be too heavy for the pony.

Too large a horse
This horse is much too large for his rider. The girl's legs do not reach far enough down his sides for her to be able to give the aids in the right place, behind the girth.

The right size
This pony and his rider are just the right size for each other. The soles of the rider's feet are level with the line of the pony's belly, so she can give the aids properly.

A variety of ponies

During your riding career you will meet many ponies. Physically, they will range from the hairy-heeled native type to the elegant, lightly-built thoroughbred type. Most will not be pure bred. Their temperaments will vary, too, from sluggish to highly excitable. Some ponies will need more experienced riders than others.

Typical beginner's pony
A first pony might be a native breed, or cross-bred. It will be quiet and dependable.

Half-bred pony
Half-bred means one of the pony's parents is a thoroughbred. This pony would suit a competent rider, and could carry out most activities.

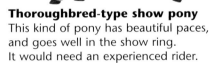

Thoroughbred-type show pony
This kind of pony has beautiful paces, and goes well in the show ring. It would need an experienced rider.

Pure-bred native pony
A pony such as this Welsh Section A (Welsh Mountain) is an ideal all-rounder for a fairly experienced rider.

A pony's tack

Tack means the saddle, bridle and other equipment used on a horse or pony. Tack is usually made from leather, with stainless steel bits and stirrups.

Saddles and girths

You need a saddle to give you a secure and comfortable seat on a horse's back. The girth holds the saddle in place. Saddles are made on a rigid frame called a tree. A canvas seat is stretched across the tree, and the padded seat goes over that. Saddles are made in different sizes and widths to fit differently sized horses.

Types of saddle

Saddles are made in different styles according to the use for which they are intended. Mostly you will use some kind of general purpose saddle, but if you go on to take part in equestrian sports you may need to use a special saddle.

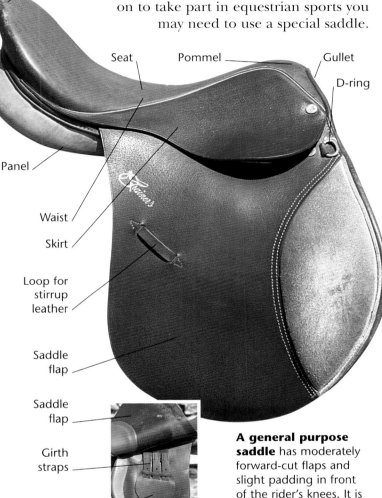

Cantle
Seat
Pommel
Gullet
D-ring
Panel
Waist
Skirt
Loop for stirrup leather
Saddle flap
Saddle flap
Girth straps
Buckle guard

A dressage saddle has straight flaps and a deep seat. It often has extended girth straps so that the buckles do not get in the way of the rider's leg contact with the horse.

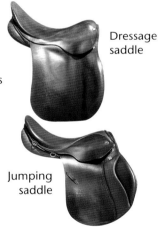

Dressage saddle

A jumping saddle has forward-cut flaps and padding in front of the rider's knees (knee rolls), and behind their thighs (thigh rolls), to help keep their legs in the right position when jumping.

Jumping saddle

A general purpose saddle has moderately forward-cut flaps and slight padding in front of the rider's knees. It is comfortable and suitable for most riding activities.

Types of girth

Girths may be made from leather, webbing, or synthetic fibres. Webbing girths were traditionally used in pairs. Leather girths, which may be made from a folded piece of leather or shaped like the Balding girth to avoid pinching near the horse's elbows, are expensive, but last a long time. String girths are cheap, but can pinch the horse's skin. Padded synthetic girths are comfortable and easy to maintain. For safety, girths should be fastened on either the front two, or the front and back, girth straps.

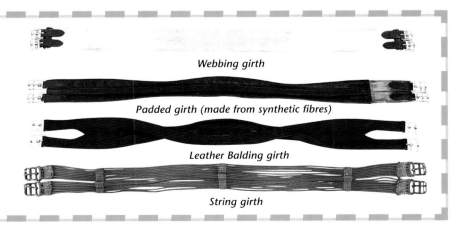

Webbing girth

Padded girth (made from synthetic fibres)

Leather Balding girth

String girth

Headcollars

Headcollars are put on horses' or ponies' heads to lead them and to tie them up. They may be made of webbing or leather. People tend to use webbing headcollars in the stable, and keep leather ones for special occasions.

The lead rope clips to the ring under the pony's chin

Bridles and bits

A bridle and bit are the means by which a horse or pony is controlled by his rider. Bridles are traditionally made of leather, in three sizes: full size, cob and pony. Other materials are also used nowadays. There are two main types of bit – snaffle and curb – though there are many different varieties. Bits are usually made of stainless steel.

Snaffle bridle

A snaffle bridle, with a jointed snaffle bit and single reins, is the kind most often used. The headpiece buckles on to cheekpieces, which hold the bit in place. A separate headpiece is attached to the noseband, and fastens on the left.

Throatlash stops the bridle from slipping forwards

Cheekpiece holds the bit in place

Noseband

Stop, to keep the ring of a running martingale away from the bit

Eggbutt snaffle bit

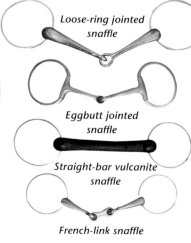

Loose-ring jointed snaffle

Eggbutt jointed snaffle

Straight-bar vulcanite snaffle

French-link snaffle

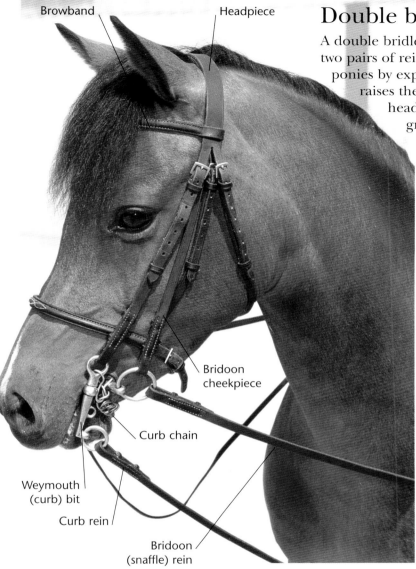

Browband

Headpiece

Bridoon cheekpiece

Curb chain

Weymouth (curb) bit

Curb rein

Bridoon (snaffle) rein

Double bridle

A double bridle has both a snaffle bit and a curb bit, and two pairs of reins. It is used only on well-schooled horses and ponies by experienced riders. The snaffle bit, or bridoon, raises the horse's head. The curb bit lowers the horse's head. The curb chain, tightening in the chin groove, gives extra control.

Roundings

Short leather straps that connect the curb and bridoon rings of a pelham bit, allowing single reins to be used with it, are called roundings. Their use means that the two functions of the bit cannot be separated, but some horses go well with them.

Running martingale

This attaches to the girth at one end. It passes through a neck strap, then divides into two straps that end in rings through which the reins pass.

Standing martingale

Like a running martingale, this also attaches to the girth and passes through a neck strap, but the single strap is then fastened to the back of the noseband of the pony's bridle.

Martingales

Martingales are used to stop a horse carrying his head too high and evading the rider's control. They also prevent him throwing his head up in the air and possibly hitting the rider in the face. They should be fitted with care. They must not be so tight that they pull the horse's head down.

Types of bit

A snaffle bit consists of a mouthpiece, usually jointed, and two rings. A curb bit has cheekpieces, which rotate to put pressure on the headpiece of the bridle. It also has a curb chain, which presses on the curb groove and is held down by a lip-strap.

A kimblewick bit, which acts like a single-rein pelham, is useful for a strong pony.

The two bits of a double bridle are the bridoon (snaffle) and Weymouth (curb).

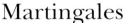

A half-moon pelham combines the actions of the snaffle and curb bits. It would be used with a curb chain.

Saddle blanket

The horse wears a thick woollen blanket or pad under the saddle to protect her back from being rubbed. Traditionally, these blankets were hand-woven from sheep's wool, and doubled as bed-rolls.

Western saddle

A traditional Western saddle weighs 18–22.5kg. Most modern saddles are lighter, but they all feature the horn at the front, to which steers were roped, and the high cantle at the back. The girth is called a cinch.

Wooden stirrup
The stirrup is made from a single, curved piece of wood. It is often covered with leather.

Horn

Cantle

Flank strap

Skirt

Fender made of decorative leather

Seat jockey

Front rigging

Western tack

Western tack was designed for a cowboy's horse. The saddle was his home. It had to be comfortable, and to carry all his belongings, from bedding and food supplies to ropes and a rifle. The bridle had long reins. When they trailed on the ground, the horse was trained to stand still, as if tied up.

Under the saddle flap
When you lift the saddle flap you can see the broad leather strap that carries the stirrup. The outer fender covers the strap and protects the rider's leg.

Putting on the saddle

If you are small, you may need help in carrying and putting on a Western saddle. It takes quite a lot of strength to lift it up on to a horse's back and settle it in place. You must never fling on the saddle, as you see in some films, because this would upset the horse.

1 First put on the saddle blanket, and then lower the saddle on to the horse's back.

2 Check the cinch is not twisted on the right side, then fasten it on the left side.

3 The cinch may be buckled or tied in place. Once you have fastened it, tuck in the free end of the leather.

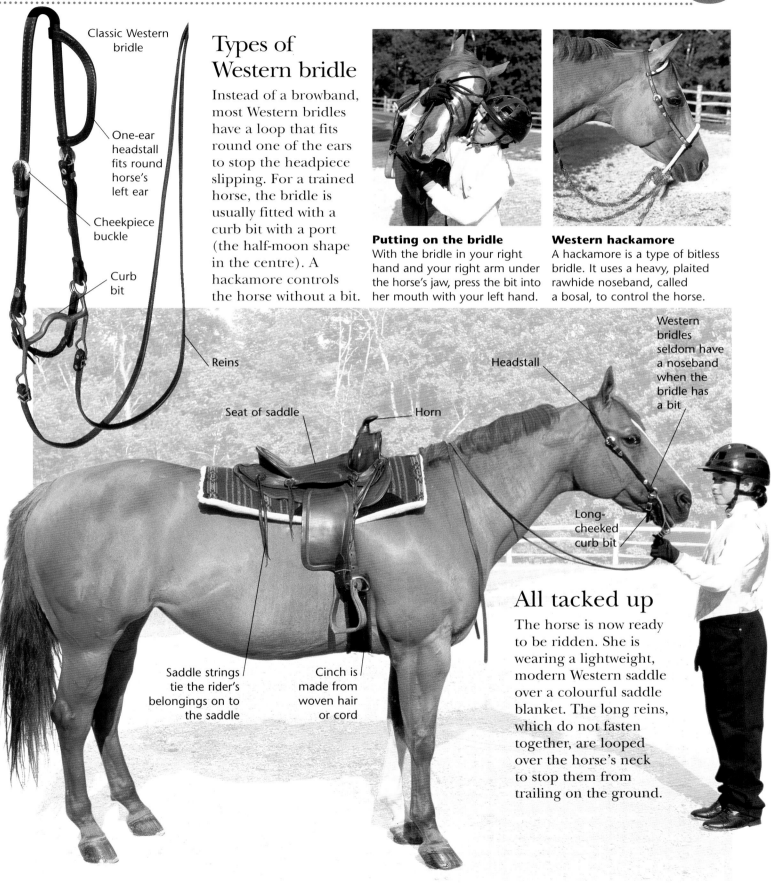

Classic Western bridle

One-ear headstall fits round horse's left ear

Cheekpiece buckle

Curb bit

Types of Western bridle

Instead of a browband, most Western bridles have a loop that fits round one of the ears to stop the headpiece slipping. For a trained horse, the bridle is usually fitted with a curb bit with a port (the half-moon shape in the centre). A hackamore controls the horse without a bit.

Putting on the bridle
With the bridle in your right hand and your right arm under the horse's jaw, press the bit into her mouth with your left hand.

Western hackamore
A hackamore is a type of bitless bridle. It uses a heavy, plaited rawhide noseband, called a bosal, to control the horse.

Reins

Seat of saddle

Horn

Headstall

Western bridles seldom have a noseband when the bridle has a bit

Long-cheeked curb bit

Saddle strings tie the rider's belongings on to the saddle

Cinch is made from woven hair or cord

All tacked up

The horse is now ready to be ridden. She is wearing a lightweight, modern Western saddle over a colourful saddle blanket. The long reins, which do not fasten together, are looped over the horse's neck to stop them from trailing on the ground.

A pony's headcollar

Headcollars are made either of leather or webbing. They are used to lead a horse or pony, and to tie it up. Like bridles, they are made in three basic sizes – pony, cob and full-size. A very small pony may need a foal headcollar, which has a number of adjustable straps.

A good fit
This leather headcollar fits well. It fastens on the pony's left side, and the lead rope is clipped to the round ring under his chin.

Too small
This headcollar was made to fit a much smaller pony. The headpiece does not even reach far enough to meet the buckle on the cheekpiece.

Too large
This headcollar is much too large. The pony could pull his head back through it and escape, or get a foot caught up in it when grazing or scratching.

Checking the size

A headcollar needs to fit correctly in the same way as a bridle does. There should be room for you to insert two fingers under the noseband, and a hand under the throatlash. A headcollar that is too tight, especially if it is made of webbing, will rub and may cause sores over the pony's prominent nasal bones.

Fitting and caring for tack

Tack is a horse's or pony's saddle, bridle, headcollar and any other saddlery he may wear, such as a martingale. To do its job properly, it must fit well, be correctly adjusted and well cared for. Neglected tack is dangerous. It can give the pony sores and may break, leading to accidents.

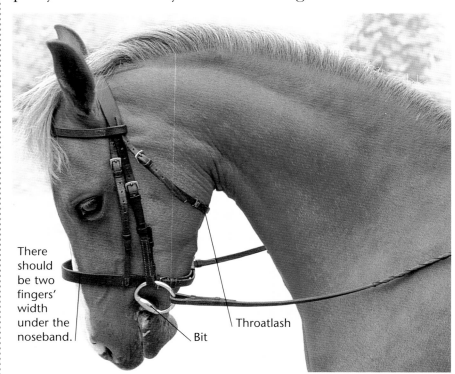

There should be two fingers' width under the noseband.

Bit

Throatlash

Well-fitting bridle

This pony is wearing a well-fitting snaffle bridle with an eggbutt snaffle bit. The browband is at the correct height so it does not pinch the pony's ears, the noseband and throatlash fit well, and the bit just wrinkles the corners of the pony's mouth.

Storing tack

Tack should be cleaned before it is put away. Bridles are hung on arched racks that do not bend the headpieces; saddles are supported on brackets fitted to the wall or on free-standing saddle horses.

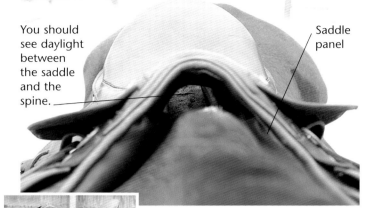

You should see daylight between the saddle and the spine.

Saddle panel

How to clean tack

It is important to keep saddle and bridle leather clean and supple. If you do so it will last for many years. You should clean it each time you use it. To clean tack, you need a bucket of warm water, one sponge for cleaning off the dirt and grease, one sponge for saddle-soaping and a bar of saddle soap.

Wash the bit in clean water and dry it. Clean all the grease and mud off the bridle with a slightly damp sponge. Then dip the bar of saddle soap into the water and rub it on to your other sponge.

Fitting a saddle

Horses and ponies vary a lot in shape and size, and it is important that the saddle fits well. It must be the right width, and the panel stuffing must be even so the leather maintains a level contact with the pony's back. The saddle must not press on the pony's spine or the withers.

Rub saddle soap well into the leather, undoing fasteners so no parts of the bridle are neglected. Keep moistening the soap when you need more on the sponge. When you have finished, refasten all the buckles.

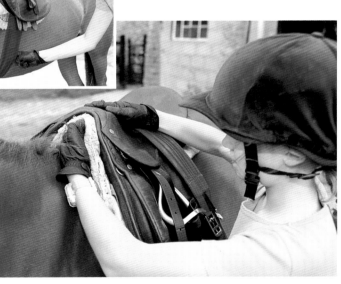

Wipe any mud off the stirrup irons with your cleaning sponge. Rinse the sponge, squeeze it as dry as possible, and clean the grease off the underside of the saddle, as well as any mud. Do not get the leather too wet.

Tacking up

Check that the numnah does not press down upon the pony's withers. You should be able to insert three fingers between the withers and the pommel of the saddle, and two between the girth and the pony.

If you wet the sponge when you are using saddle soap, you will have too much lather. Moisten the soap instead. Rub the sponge all over the saddle. Don't forget the girth straps and stirrup leathers.

Tying a quick-release knot

When tying up a pony, fasten his rope to a loop of string, using a quick-release knot for untying in an emergency.

Loop the lead rope and put it through the string loop. Twist the rope a few times.

Make another loop in the end of the rope and push it through the first loop.

Tighten the knot by pulling on the headcollar end. Pull the free end to undo it.

Putting on a headcollar

You will need to put a headcollar on a pony in the stable so you can tie him up while you are grooming, tacking up and mucking out. You will also need to use a headcollar to catch him and lead him back from the field to the stable.

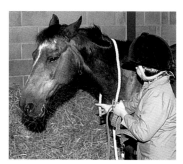

1 If the pony is outside, or if he is likely to wander around the loose box, first put the lead rope round his neck so you can hold on to him if you need to do so.

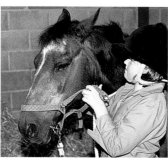

2 Put the noseband over his nose. Hold the cheekpiece of the headcollar in your left hand. Reach under his chin with your right hand to grasp the headpiece.

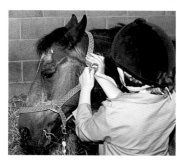

3 Bring the headpiece over the pony's head and fasten the buckle, tucking in the end of the strap. Tie up the pony using a quick-release knot.

Saddling up

When you have your first riding lessons, your pony will be already tacked up – that is, he will have his saddle and bridle on. But you will need to learn how to do this for yourself. Start by tying him up in the stable, then fetch his tack. You can hang the bridle on a hook or over the door while you saddle the pony.

Carry the bridle over your shoulder

Carry the saddle over your arm with the pommel resting by your elbow

Run the stirrups up the leathers

Carry the girth over the saddle

Carrying tack

To avoid trailing the reins on the ground, loop them up and put them with the bridle over your shoulder. Carry the saddle on your left arm, supporting it with your right hand. It is then in position for saddling the pony.

Putting on a saddle

The saddle sits just behind the pony's withers, and the girth goes round in the shallow groove just behind his forelegs. You put the saddle on from the pony's left side, but you must go round to the right side to fasten on the numnah and to check that the girth is correctly buckled on that side and not twisted.

1 Hold the numnah in both hands, and lower it on to the pony's back, in front of where it will eventually go.

2 Put the saddle on top of the numnah, then slide them back together until they are in the right position.

3 Take the front girth strap out of the buckle guard and slide it through the loop on the numnah's strap.

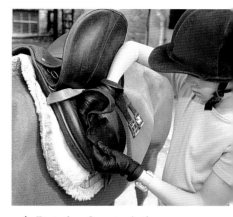

4 Put the front girth strap back through the buckle guard. Repeat steps three and four on the left of the saddle.

5 Let the girth hang down on the right side and check that it is not twisted.

6 Go back to the left side of the pony and reach underneath his belly to get hold of the end of the girth.

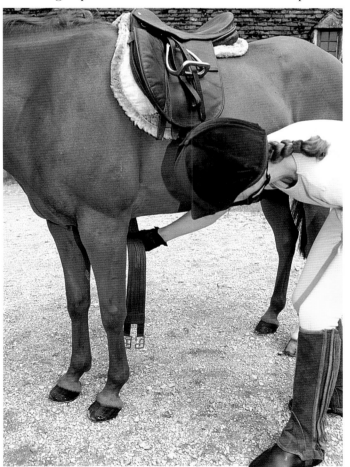

7 Fasten the girth buckles on the front two or the front and back girth straps. Smooth the skin under the girth.

Slide the guard back down over the girth buckles.

Putting on a bridle

A horse's or pony's head is very sensitive, so you must always handle it gently when putting on his bridle. Take care not to brush your arm or the bridle's cheekpieces against his eyes. Do not pull on his mouth when you put in the bit. If you do it slowly and methodically, putting on a bridle is not as difficult as it may appear.

How to put on a bridle

When you are learning, a bridle appears to be a very complicated piece of equipment. The key to being able to put it on without getting in a muddle is to hold it up by the headpiece and take a good look at it. The headpiece goes over the top of the pony's head, and the cheekpieces support the bit. The browband stops the headpiece slipping backwards, and the throatlash stops the bridle slipping forwards.

1 Carrying the bridle, approach the pony on his left side and undo his headcollar. Slip it off his head and then refasten the headpiece round his neck.

Checking the fit

A horse or pony usually wears the same bridle each time he is ridden, so it should fit him properly without much adjustment. But you need to know how the bridle should fit to be sure it is correct.

Before you put on the bridle, check that the noseband is level. If it is not, straighten it by easing its headpiece through the browband, pushing it up on one side and pulling it down on the other.

The cheekpieces should be buckled on to the bridle's headpiece at the same number hole on each side. If they are not, the bit will be pulled up more on one side than on the other.

When the noseband is fitted correctly, it should lie midway between the pony's cheekbone and his mouth. There should be enough room for you to slide two fingers between the noseband and the pony's nose.

When you have fastened the throatlash, there should be room for your whole hand to pass between it and the pony's cheek. If the throatlash is too tight it may interfere with the pony's breathing.

A snaffle bit should slightly wrinkle the corners of a pony's mouth when it is at the correct height. You can adjust the height of the bit by altering the length of the cheekpieces on each side of the bridle.

6 Pull out the pony's forelock from under the browband so it lies tidily over it. Smooth out any parts of the mane that are caught up in the headpiece.

2 Hold the bridle in your left hand by the headpiece. Take hold of the reins in your right hand and put them over the pony's neck.

3 Put your right arm under the pony's jaw and hold the bridle in your right hand. Holding the bit flat on your outstretched left hand, press it against the pony's lips.

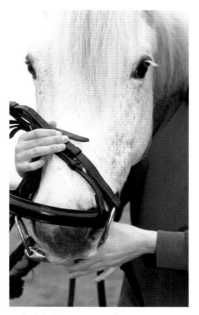

4 If the pony does not want to open his mouth, wiggle your left thumb in the corner where he has no teeth. Press the bit against his lips as you do so.

5 When the bit is in the pony's mouth, put the bridle's headpiece over his ears, folding the ears down to enable you to do so.

7 On both sides of the bridle, check that the browband is not fitted so high up that it is pressing against the base of the pony's ears.

8 Reach under the pony's jaw to the right-hand side of the bridle for the throatlash. Check it is not twisted, then bring it round to the left side of the bridle and fasten the buckle.

9 Check that the bridle's noseband is not caught up on the cheekpieces, then fasten it behind the pony's jaw. Push the end of the noseband strap firmly through its keeper.

10 Do a final check on the bridle. Make sure the buckles are fastened properly and the ends of all the straps are in their keepers.

First lessons

The first time you sit on a pony you will probably feel a little strange. As you have more lessons you will begin to feel at home on his back. Your first pony will be a very quiet one, and he will help your instructor to take care of you.

Meeting your pony

When you go for your first riding lesson, your instructor will introduce you to the pony you are going to ride. It is a very exciting moment – although you may feel a bit nervous. If you do, try to hide it from the pony. Ponies quickly sense how someone is feeling and react to it. If you are anxious and upset, or worried, your pony will become anxious, too. If you act in a positive way, your pony will have confidence in you.

Greeting a new friend

When you meet a strange pony, walk up to him confidently. Hold out the back of your hand with your fingers curled into your palm, and let him sniff at it. Speak to him, and give him a pat on the neck.

Getting ready

If you are having a group lesson, the ponies will be brought out into the stable yard for their riders to mount. Before you mount, you or your instructor should check the pony's tack. Your instructor will probably help you mount by holding the pony.

Setting off

When all the riders have mounted their ponies, and checked their girths and the length of their stirrups (see pages 154–155), the ride will leave the yard and set out for the outdoor or the indoor school.

Your first lessons

You may have individual riding lessons, or lessons with a group of other beginners. Either way, your instructor, or an assistant, will probably lead your pony with a leading rein. This clips on to the pony's bit rings, leaving you to hold the bridle's reins.

Getting to know a pony

Before you can handle and ride ponies, you need to know a bit about them. Ponies are gentle, nervous animals, happiest in a group. If something frightens them, their instinct is to run away. Living naturally, in a herd, they follow a dominant pony. When we domesticate them, we take that animal's place, and once they trust us, they will do as we wish.

Approach with confidence

When you approach a pony, talk to him in a friendly way. Give him a pat on the neck or a titbit, and handle him quietly and firmly. He will then feel confident. If you are nervous, hesitant or bullying, he will be upset and may behave badly.

How to lead a pony correctly

You lead a pony on his left side. Hold the lead rope or reins in your right hand up by the pony's head, and take the other end in your left hand. Walk forwards in a positive way beside the pony's shoulder without looking back at him.

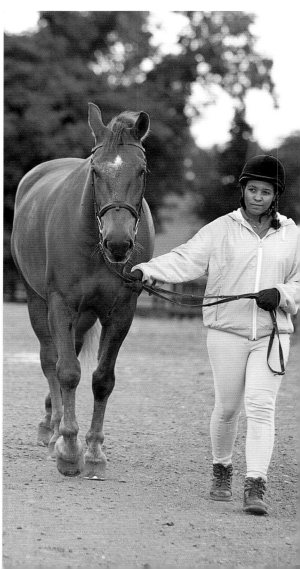

Natural behaviour

Wild ponies live together in herds. If you turn a pony out in a field, he will immediately gallop off to join the others. If one pony shies at an object, the others will copy him.

Nervous or naughty?

A pony that hesitates about passing an unusual object may be frightened, or may be playing you up. Give him the benefit of the doubt and let him have a good look at it. Then drive him firmly forwards with your seat and legs, keeping on the pressure until he has gone past the object.

Gaining control

Once the pony walks past the object, relax your aids, and make a fuss of him. Pat him on the neck and tell him he is a good boy. If he refuses to pass the object, take him round in a circle and approach it again, reinforcing your aids with a whip if necessary.

Mounting block

A mounting block gives you extra height and stops you pulling the saddle over.

Hold the reins in your left hand and put your left foot in the stirrup. Spring off your right foot, with your right hand holding the saddle.

Swing your right leg over the horse's back and lower yourself into the saddle. Put your right foot in the stirrup, then take up the right rein.

Getting a leg up

Hold the reins in your left hand and put your right hand on the saddle. Your helper holds your left leg.

With your helper supporting your left leg below the knee, decide when he or she will lift, such as on the count of three. Lift yourself with your arms while your helper propels you up.

When you reach the level of the saddle, swing your right leg over it and sit down. Straighten your back, put both your feet in the stirrups, then take up the reins in both hands.

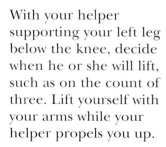

Mounting

Mounting means getting on a horse or pony. Although you may have help at first, you will need to manage alone. When you are out riding, you may have to dismount to open a gate, for example, and you must be able to get back on again. If you find mounting difficult because you are not very athletic and lack spring, or because you are not very tall, try letting the stirrup leather down a hole or two.

How to mount

There are various ways of mounting a pony. You may be able to use a mounting block or to get a leg up in the riding school, but you will also be taught the correct way to mount. When you are learning, you should have a helper to hold your pony. When you are on your own, you can stop him from walking forwards by standing him to face a wall or gate.

1 Stand on the pony's left side facing his tail. Hold the reins in your left hand. With your right hand, turn the stirrup towards you, and put your left foot in it.

2 With your left hand resting on the pony's withers, grasp the waist of the saddle with your right hand and at the same time spring up off your right foot.

Turning the stirrup

It is important that the stirrup iron and leather are turned the right way when you are riding. If they are not, the edge of the stirrup leather presses into your leg. This is not only very uncomfortable, it prevents you from using your legs properly.

Before you mount, turn the back of the stirrup iron towards you. As you mount and twist your leg and foot round, the stirrup turns so it ends up facing the right way.

To put your right foot in the stirrup, turn the front of the iron outwards. You may do this with your hand at first, but with practice you will be able to use your foot.

Western style

Start by facing the horse's left side. Hold the reins in your left hand, resting on the horn of the saddle. Put your left foot in the stirrup and your right hand on the back of the saddle. Spring up off your right foot. Swing your right leg over, taking care not to catch it on the high cantle. Lower yourself gently into the saddle. Put your right foot in the stirrup and take the reins in your right hand.

3 Swing your right leg up and over the pony's back, taking care you do not kick him with your toe as you do so. It is helpful if someone leans on your right stirrup as you mount to stop you from pulling the saddle over to the left when all your weight is on that side.

4 As you bring your right leg over the saddle, slide your right hand out of the way. Lower yourself down gently, do not flop.

5 Slip your right foot into the right stirrup, pointing your toe inwards as you do so. Take up the reins in both your hands.

Dismounting

The method of dismounting that starts with both feet out of the stirrups involves a certain amount of gymnastics. Most people consider it is the best way to get off a horse because it is the safest. The most dangerous thing that can happen to a rider is to be dragged along the ground by a moving horse because one foot is stuck in a stirrup. By taking both feet out of the stirrups and then jumping clear, you land on both feet together, and can walk on with the horse.

How to dismount

When dismounting, you vault off the pony in one easy movement, so you have both feet on the ground very quickly and can walk beside the pony if he moves. As you land beside the pony, be careful to keep your own feet out of the way of his front hooves so he does not tread on you. Before you dismount, check that you are not going to land on uneven ground and risk hurting your feet or ankles as they take your weight.

1 Bring the pony up to a good square halt (see page 160) on a level piece of ground. If you think he may walk forwards, face a gate. Still keeping hold of the reins in both hands, take both feet out of the stirrups.

1 Hold the reins in your left hand and put your right hand on the pommel. Then take your right foot out of the stirrup.

Alternative way

An alternative method is to take your right foot out of the stirrup first, then vault off to land on both feet together. Unless the pony is trained to stand, you should get someone to hold him while you dismount this way.

2 Pass the reins, and whip if you are using one, to your left hand. Rest them on the base of the pony's neck, just in front of the withers.

2 Swing your right leg over the pony's back and put your right hand on the waist of the saddle. Take your left foot out of the stirrup and vault off.

3 Slip to the ground, landing on both feet and bending your knees slightly as you do so. Then, with your right hand, take hold of the reins by the bit so you can lead him.

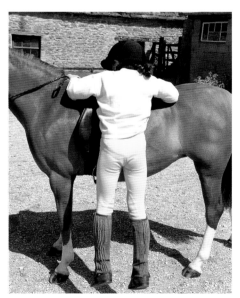

3 While still keeping hold of the reins in your left hand, put your right hand on the pommel of the saddle and lean forwards.

4 Swing your right leg up and bring it over the pony's back, taking care that you do not kick him as you do so.

5 Slip to the ground, landing lightly on both feet and bending your knees. Take hold of the reins near the bit in your right hand.

How to sit in the saddle

W hen you sit on a horse or a pony you should be relaxed and comfortable, yet alert and ready for action. You should sit well down in the saddle, with your back straight and your thighs and lower legs in contact with the saddle and the pony. Your body should be supple enough to follow all his movements.

How to hold the reins

Hold your hands in a relaxed position in front of you with the thumbs uppermost and the palms of your hands facing each other. Then take up the reins. Single reins should pass between your third and fourth fingers, up through your hands, and between your thumbs and first fingers.

Diagonal line

When you are sitting on the pony your arms must be in the right position. If you are holding the reins correctly, the reins and the lower parts of your arms should form a straight, diagonal line running directly from the pony's bit back to your elbows.

Shortening reins

Hold both reins in your right hand while you slide your left hand down to the length you want. Then hold both reins in your left hand and slide your right hand down to shorten the right rein to the correct length.

Foot position in stirrup
When you are putting your foot in the stirrup, turn the front edge of the iron outwards. Rest the ball of your foot on the stirrup iron and keep your toes pointing forwards and your heels pressed down.

Stirrup length

If you sit in the saddle and let your legs hang down naturally, the stirrups will be approximately the correct length when the treads of the irons are level with the insteps of your feet. You may need them a couple of holes shorter than this to start with, and when jumping.

Keep your head up and look straight ahead between the pony's ears

Sit up straight, but do not hold your back stiffly

Keep your upper arms relaxed and hold them close to your body

Keep your seat in contact with the saddle and do not lean back

Keep your heels down and your toes up

Vertical line

When you are sitting in the saddle, imagine a straight vertical line running down beside you. If you are sitting in the correct position, the line would start at your ear and pass down through your shoulder and hip, before eventually finishing at the level of your heel.

Checking the girth

You should check the girth before you mount, but it is a good idea to check it again after a few minutes' riding. Some ponies blow themselves out when they are saddled and their girths are being tightened. Later, when they have relaxed, the girth may be too loose. You can adjust it from either side.

Keeping hold of the reins, lean forwards to slide your fingers under the girth. If you can get more than two fingers between the girth and the pony, then you need to tighten the girth.

Put your left leg forwards, lift the saddle flap and pull up the girth straps one at a time to tighten them.

Adjusting the stirrup length

You can adjust your stirrups when in the saddle, keeping your feet in them as you do so. With a bit of practice, you can do this by feel alone, without looking down.

Holding the reins in one hand, pull up the end of the leather with the other.

Undo the buckle, slide it to the correct position and put the prong in the hole.

Pull down the underneath part of the leather to slide the buckle up again.

The aids

The aids are the signals by which a rider communicates his or her wishes to a horse or pony. The aids are divided into natural aids – the rider's legs, hands, seat and voice – and artificial aids – whips and spurs. A well-trained horse responds to the lightest of aids, but a first pony may need stronger ones.

Hand position
Keep your fingers closed while you keep an even contact with the horse's mouth.

Boot with spur fitted

Spurs are attached to riding boots with leather straps.

Artificial aids

Schooling whip

Riding whip

Riding whip

There are various kinds of whip. Long whips are used for dressage and schooling; short whips for ordinary riding; and canes, which may be leather-covered, for showing. Both whips and spurs are used to reinforce leg aids, although spurs should be used only by experienced riders.

Hand position
Let your fingers relax and keep a loose hold on the reins.

Riding on a loose rein

At the end of a ride, and at intervals during a schooling period, it is a good idea to let the horse walk on a loose rein to stretch his neck muscles and relax. When you are riding on a loose rein, you still need to keep your lower legs in contact with the horse's sides, but you can ease the pressure on the reins. However, you must always be ready to gather up the reins quickly if something startles the horse.

Medium walk

Maintain a feel on the horse's mouth through the reins. With your lower legs, squeeze his sides behind the girth to tell him to walk forwards.

Leg position
Keep your heels well down and your lower legs pressed into the horse's sides.

Driving forwards

Sometimes ponies dislike or are afraid of particular objects, and refuse to pass them. When this happens, keep a firm hold of the reins and use your legs really strongly to drive the pony forwards.

Using a whip

If the pony does not pay attention to your leg aid, you can reinforce it with a tap of the whip just behind the girth. A pony that behaves badly can also be given a sharp tap with the whip in the same place.

Expert rider

If you watch an expert rider performing a dressage test you will hardly notice any aids being given. The lightest of touches and slight shifts of weight in the saddle are enough to instruct the horse to carry out the most complicated movements.

A dressage rider rides with long stirrups. This is Nancy MacLachlan in 1998.

This dressage movement is called a piaffe. It is like trotting on the spot.

'Leg into hand' is the aim of riding. The legs drive the horse forwards; the hands control the energy created.

First-time rider

On the leading rein, the instructor has direct control of the pony. To help the rider feel safe on her first lesson, the instructor will tell her to hold on to the front of the saddle or a neck strap.

On the lunge or leading rein

Your first few riding lessons are likely to be on the lunge or on a leading rein. The instructor controls your pony, leaving you free to concentrate on sitting correctly and applying the aids. A lunge line is a long rein attached to a special headcollar, which the pony wears over his bridle.

Starting out
As the horse walks round in circles, the rider steadies herself by holding on to the front of the saddle.

Gaining confidence
Once the rider feels secure, she lets go of the saddle and holds the reins in the correct position.

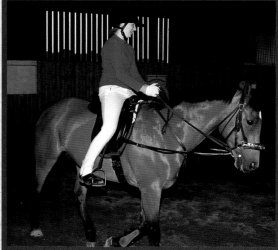

On the lunge

Riding on the lunge is a good way of learning to balance on the horse and to build up your confidence. It enables you to practise using the aids without having to worry about the horse's speed or direction.

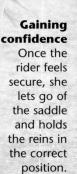

Tips for first lessons

Get comfortable in the saddle before you start. Make sure that your stirrups feel right, and that the ends of the leathers are not sticking into your legs.

If you feel insecure, hold on to the front of the saddle, or to a neck strap.

Try to relax. Let your hands follow the movement of the pony's head.

Off balance

If you lose your balance when you are first learning to ride, it is tempting to try to hang on by pulling on the reins. You should never do so, however, as you can damage the pony's mouth and may make it very sore.

Trying too hard

When you first ride a horse or pony you must try to remember many things, but do not try so hard that you hold your body stiffly. Try to sit easily and let your body and hands follow the horse's movements.

Holding the reins
You can rest your hands on either side of the horse's withers to help you balance

Headcollar
The horse may wear a headcollar to lead him by

Using your legs
Squeeze with your legs behind the girth to keep the horse walking on

Walking slowly
At first, the instructor will lead the horse round at a slow walk

On your own

W hen you first ride off the lunge or leading
rein, you will learn how to make your pony
walk on and halt. This is not as easy as it sounds.
The aim is to make the pony walk purposefully
and with energy, and to halt when you tell him
to do so. He should be balanced, alert and
responsive to your aids at all times.

Square halt

To achieve a good, square halt, with
the horse's forelegs and hind legs
in line, you have to drive him
forwards with your legs, then halt
him with the reins. Although he
is standing still, he should be
full of contained energy, and
ready to move off again.

Keep a contact
Although you have stopped, keep your legs against the pony's sides and keep a feel on the reins

Hind legs
A gentle nudge with your own leg will make the pony move his hind leg on that side into line

Front legs
As you ride forwards into halt, try to make sure that the front legs are in line

Not listening

Some ponies ignore their rider's
aids. Riders do not always give
strong enough aids for their
ponies, which then plod along
sleepily with their noses stuck
out. Applying the legs more
strongly and shortening the reins
will improve the pony's paces.

Balanced
The pony is well balanced and ready to walk on again when you ask him to do so

Working on the bit

When you are riding a horse or pony he should always be 'on the bit'. This means that his head is held vertically and his mouth is below the level of the rider's hands. In this position, the rider has the best possible control over the horse. It can be difficult to achieve and maintain, especially for an inexperienced rider and a pony that may not be perfectly schooled, but you can do it with practice.

Head position
The pony is holding his head just behind the vertical, but he is striding out well

Walk to halt, and halt to walk

This movement is achieved by pressure from your legs and on the reins. Although your lower legs, and your hands via the reins, should always be in contact with the pony, increasing or decreasing that contact tells him what you want him to do. Once he has obeyed your aids, you should relax them.

1 To ask a pony to walk on, put slight pressure on the reins and squeeze his sides with your lower legs behind the girth. As he obeys, relax the reins and the leg aid slightly.

2 To halt, increase the pressure with your legs, so driving the pony forwards into the bit. To stop him from moving forwards, resist the movement with your hands and the reins.

3 Try to get the pony to halt squarely. Although you have stopped, do not completely relax your position. Maintain contact with your legs and hands to keep the pony alert.

4 To move off into walk again, press your legs more firmly into the pony's sides and relax the reins a little to let him walk forwards. Then relax your aids, but maintain contact.

Turning left and right

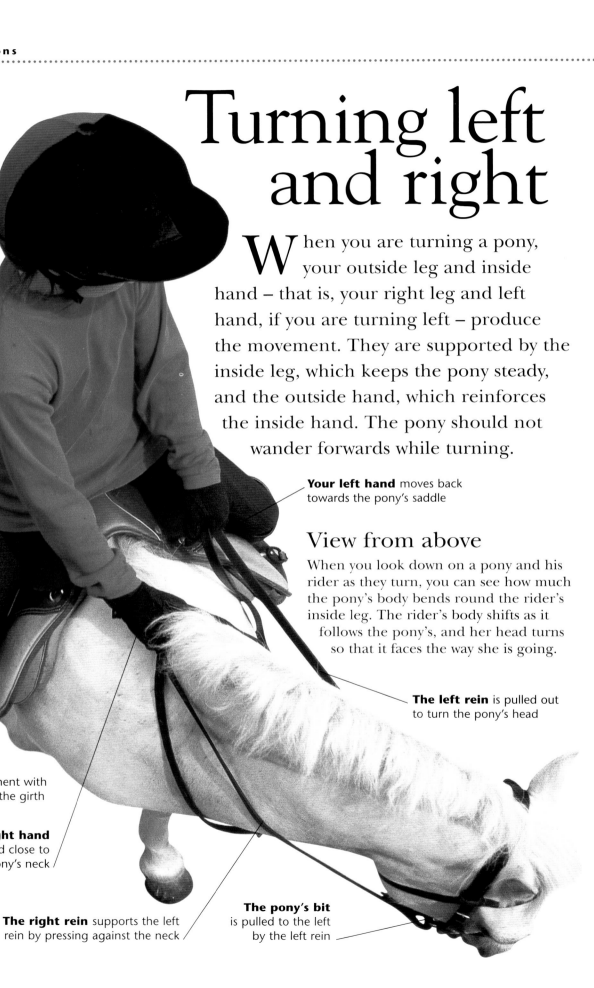

When you are turning a pony, your outside leg and inside hand – that is, your right leg and left hand, if you are turning left – produce the movement. They are supported by the inside leg, which keeps the pony steady, and the outside hand, which reinforces the inside hand. The pony should not wander forwards while turning.

Your left hand moves back towards the pony's saddle

View from above

When you look down on a pony and his rider as they turn, you can see how much the pony's body bends round the rider's inside leg. The rider's body shifts as it follows the pony's, and her head turns so that it faces the way she is going.

The left rein is pulled out to turn the pony's head

Your right leg starts the movement with pressure behind the girth

Your right hand is held close to the pony's neck

The right rein supports the left rein by pressing against the neck

The pony's bit is pulled to the left by the left rein

1 Starting from halt, press your right leg into the pony's side behind the girth and feel your left rein.

Turning left

When you are turning left, the pony's forelegs and right hind leg move round his left hind leg. As soon as you have completed the turn, you should drive the pony forwards to walk or trot in a straight line.

2 Keep your left leg on the girth. Bring the right rein over to press on the pony's neck.

3 As he starts to turn, the pony's forelegs move in a semi-circle round his hind legs.

4 Continue to apply your hand and leg aids until you have turned the pony as far as you want to go.

1 Begin by pressing your left leg against the pony's side just behind the girth.

Turning right

In a turn to the right, the pony's forelegs and left hind leg move round his right hind leg. His neck and his spine bend in the direction of the movement.

2 Feel the right rein to turn the pony's head by bringing your hand out slightly.

3 Move your left hand towards the right to press the left rein against the pony's neck.

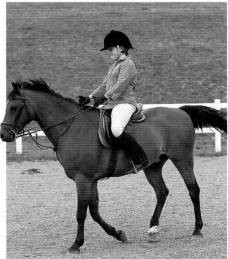

4 Continue to drive the pony round with your left leg. Try not to let him step forwards as he turns.

Practising rising to the trot

Before you learn to trot, practise rising with the horse standing still. Take your weight on your feet in the stirrups, stand for a moment, then sit down again. If you feel unsteady, rest your hands on the front of the saddle or on the horse's withers.

Stand up in the stirrups, keeping your knees slightly bent and taking your weight on the balls of your feet.

Lower yourself gently down to sit back in the saddle again. Do not let yourself flop down with a bump.

Learning to trot

The trot is a two-beat pace in which the pony's legs move in diagonal pairs: left fore and right hind, right fore and left hind. Because of this, it is very bumpy for the rider. To even out the bumps, you rise to the trot most of the time. But for more advanced riding, you also have to learn to sit to the trot. This is more difficult to do.

Rising trot

To rise to the trot you take your weight off the saddle by standing in the stirrups as one pair of the pony's legs moves forwards. Then sit down again as the opposite pair of legs moves. Try not to rise too high. At first, it is difficult to get the rhythm right.

Changing the diagonal

When you rise to the trot you are said to be riding on either the right or the left diagonal, according to which pair of the pony's feet touches the ground as you sit in the saddle. To change the diagonal, you simply sit for an extra beat and then continue rising again. You should change the diagonal when you change the rein, and every so often when out hacking.

On the left diagonal the rider sits in the saddle as the pony's left forefoot and right hind foot hit the ground. Most people ride on the left diagonal when they are trotting a circle to the right.

On the right diagonal the rider sits in the saddle as the pony's right forefoot and left hind foot hit the ground. Most people ride on the right diagonal when they are trotting a circle to the left.

Sitting trot

To sit to the trot, you must keep your bottom and your thighs in contact with the saddle all the time and not bump about. You need good balance to do this, and you must relax the lower part of your back and allow it to absorb the pony's movements.

Transitions

A change of pace is called a transition. Going faster is an upward transition, going more slowly is a downward transition. To carry out transitions successfully you need impulsion, which is the energy you create in the pony by using the aids.

From walk . . .
Start with a good walk, with the pony striding forwards full of energy. To ask for trot, take a firmer contact on your reins and squeeze with your legs behind the girth. As the pony begins to move forwards into trot, ease your aids.

. . . to trot
As the pony starts to trot, relax your reins a little to allow him to move forwards, but maintain a contact. If he seems to want to go back to walk, you will need to re-apply your legs to keep him going. If necessary, use a whip.

Trot on
Once the pony gets into his stride you need to keep him trotting with a good, even rhythm. Keep a contact with your hands and legs. How strong this contact must be will depend on how forward-going the pony is.

From trot . . .
To carry out a downward transition from trot to walk, sit down in the saddle and squeeze with your legs behind the girth to drive the pony forwards into his bit. At the same time, resist the forward movement with your hands.

. . . back to walk
When the pony slows down to walk, relax your aids but still maintain contact with your legs and hands. You may still need to drive him forwards to get a good, free-striding walk, and you still need to maintain impulsion.

Canter on

The canter is a lovely pace once you have learned how to sit to it. At first you will bump out of the saddle, which is uncomfortable. To sit to the canter, you must keep in contact with the saddle, and at the same time try to relax.

The aids

To canter with the right leg leading, squeeze with your left leg behind the girth and feel your right rein. Keep your right leg pressed into the pony on the girth. Reverse the aids in order to canter with the left leg leading.

Keep your back straight

Sit well down in the saddle

Left leg gives aid for canter right

Tips for cantering

Before you give the aids for canter, the pony must be going forwards well and be balanced. This will be in trot when you are learning. You must drive him forwards with your legs and control the energy with your hands, not let him trot faster and faster and become unbalanced.

Try to relax the lower part of your back when you canter, so you can follow the pony's movements.

Do not lean forwards out of the saddle, because the pony may interpret this as a signal to go faster.

Keep your reins fairly short and maintain contact with the pony's mouth so he cannot get his head down.

The pony should be light on his feet when he is cantering

The gait

The canter is a three-beat pace, in which the horse's fore- and hind legs on one side are in advance of those on the other. The horse is said to be leading with, or on, the right or the left leg. When he is leading with the right leg, his feet hit the ground in the following sequence: left hind, right hind and left fore together, right fore. After this, there is a moment of suspension when all the feet are off the ground at the same time. A well-schooled horse can change the leading leg while in the air. This is called a flying change.

Good working canter

The working canter is the pace you will learn when you first start cantering. Travelling at average speed, the pony should move freely with a good rhythm, and respond to your aids at all times.

Keep a good contact on the reins so that you stay in control

Keep the pony cantering with pressure from your right leg

The pony's weight is on his left foreleg and right hind leg

This pony is cantering with his right leg leading

Checking leading leg

You should be able to feel which leg is leading in canter because the pony's shoulder on that side will be slightly in advance of his other shoulder. But when you are first learning, you may need to take a quick look down to check.

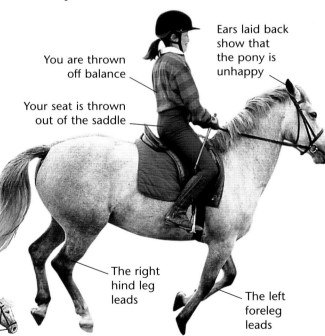

Ears laid back show that the pony is unhappy

You are thrown off balance

Your seat is thrown out of the saddle

The right hind leg leads

The left foreleg leads

Right fore leading
The right hind and left fore are just hitting the ground.

Right fore leading
All the pony's weight is now taken on the right foreleg.

In the air
For a brief moment all the pony's legs are in the air.

Cantering disunited

When a pony leads with one front leg and the opposite hind leg in canter he is said to be cantering disunited. It is uncomfortable for both the pony and the rider. If it happens, go back to trot and give the aids for canter again.

Riding at top speed

Galloping is very exciting for both pony and rider. Do not attempt it until you are sure you can control your pony in canter. Choose a good place to gallop. A smooth field with an uphill slope is ideal – it is easier to stop when going uphill! Never gallop over rough ground, near or up to other ponies, or in a confined space. Make sure there is plenty of room to manoeuvre.

Forward position

When you gallop you should go into 'forward position'. This means leaning forwards and taking your weight on your knees and feet. Raise your bottom just clear of the saddle, but keep in balance. Practise the position first in halt.

Asking for gallop

Get your pony into a good canter and take up the forward position. Urge her forwards with your legs until you are going fast enough for the canter to become a gallop. Keep contact with her mouth through the reins.

The gallop

The gallop is the fastest pace. It is a four-beat pace, with each foot hitting the ground separately. When the left foreleg is leading, the sequence is right hind, left hind, right fore and left fore.

Body position
When you are in forward position, keep your head up and look where you are going

Suspension
There is a moment in gallop when all four feet are off the ground

Slowing down

Ponies love to gallop, and they can be difficult to stop. When you want to slow down to canter, maintain contact with your legs and take an upright position again. Resist the forward movement with the reins until the pony responds.

Fast forward

The average pony probably gallops at about 24km/h. This may not sound very fast, but when you are thundering along with the wind whistling past your ears, it certainly feels it! The Thoroughbred is the fastest horse in the world. It gallops at about 50km/h, but its record race speed is an amazing 69.2km/h over 0.4km.

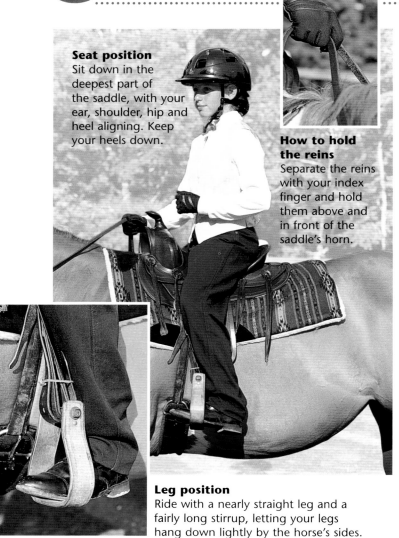

Seat position
Sit down in the deepest part of the saddle, with your ear, shoulder, hip and heel aligning. Keep your heels down.

How to hold the reins
Separate the reins with your index finger and hold them above and in front of the saddle's horn.

Leg position
Ride with a nearly straight leg and a fairly long stirrup, letting your legs hang down lightly by the horse's sides.

Western riding

When riding Western-style you use only the lightest of touches to tell the horse what to do. When he has obeyed your aids and is carrying out your wishes, you sit still and do nothing. You do not need to keep in contact with his mouth, but hold the reins very lightly, except when giving specific aids. You use your voice as an aid to tell him to move forwards at different paces, and to halt.

Legs, seat and hands

You should sit up tall and straight in the saddle, yet be in a relaxed position. Rest the balls of your feet in the stirrups. You hold your hands higher than you would in English-style riding, at approximately the level of your elbows. When you are riding Western-style, you may hold the reins in one hand or two, except in competitions.

Turning left

Giving the aids for turning with the reins in one hand only is called neck-reining. The rein on the inside of the turn makes the horse look in the direction she is going. The rein on the outside puts pressure on her neck, telling her to move over.

1 Move your right hand to the left, so the left rein turns the horse's head in the correct direction and the right rein presses against her neck.

2 Look in the direction in which you want to go. At the same time, relax your left leg and push the horse over to the left with your right leg.

Turning right

When you are turning right, the right rein turns the horse's head to the right, and the left rein presses against her neck to tell her to move to the right. Your right leg relaxes and your left leg pushes the horse over.

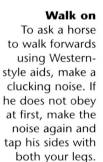

1 The right rein starts the movement, and the left rein presses against the horse's neck.

2 Look towards the right and push the horse over with your left leg until the turn is completed.

Walk, jog, halt

Western riding is based on a system of ask and release. You ask the horse to move forwards or stop using your voice, reinforced by your legs and reins if necessary. As soon as he obeys, you relax the aids. This release is his reward. As the horse moves into a faster pace, his head will rise. As it does this, take up some of the slack in the reins, but do not pull on the horse's mouth.

Walk on
To ask a horse to walk forwards using Western-style aids, make a clucking noise. If he does not obey at first, make the noise again and tap his sides with both your legs.

Western jog
This is a kind of slow trot. Ask the horse for it with the clucking noise, reinforced with your leg aids if necessary, and shorten the reins slightly as the horse's head rises.

To halt
Push your weight down into your heels and brace your body, while saying, "Whoa." If the horse does not obey, raise your reins a little to put pressure on the bit. Repeat the rein aid if necessary.

In the school

When you have learned how to ride at the basic paces, and can control a pony on your own, you will progress to carrying out various exercises in the riding school. These will improve your skills and make you a better rider.

A group lesson in the school
In a group lesson, you have to keep up with the pace of the pony in front of you, and keep your pony's mind on his work.

Passing shoulder to shoulder

While you are riding in the school you may have to ride past another pony and rider. When you do this, you should pass left shoulder to left shoulder. This is also the generally accepted way of passing another rider you may meet when out hacking.

Riding at the correct distance

When you are riding in a group you must leave a pony's length between your pony and the pony in front of you. Riding close up behind another pony may upset it, and it might kick out at your own pony and injure it, or you.

Riding in a group

Riding in a group can be quite a challenge at first. There are many things to remember. You must control your own pony, but at the same time consider what other riders are doing. Your pony may behave differently, too, in the company of others. He may be more excitable, or he may refuse to leave the other ponies to carry out your wishes. You will learn both from your own riding, and from watching others.

Exercises in the school

C arrying out individual exercises in the riding school that involve changes of pace and direction, such as riding circles and loops, is a good way of testing your riding ability. You must manage your pony and give the correct aids at the right time. Your instructor will help you if you need advice.

Riding exercises in pairs

If you have four or more riders in your group you can carry out exercises in pairs. This is fun to do, but it is a great test of timing and judgment. You must keep level with each other all the time, which is difficult if one pony has a longer stride than the other. You might ride up the school, circle in opposite directions, then pair up again. With practice, you can do this at trot and canter.

Dressage arena

Most riding schools are marked out with letters like a dressage arena. You can use the letters as points at which to change your direction or pace. For example, you might walk from K to H, trot to F, and so on. To remember the sequence of the letters, use a phrase like 'All King Edward's Horses Can Make Big Fences'.

C

H   M

E   B | 40m

K   F

A

← 20m →

Changing pace

If you are told you must walk to H and then trot to M, you should break into a trot as your pony's shoulder becomes level with the letter. It is quite a challenge, and your pony must be well-balanced and obedient to your aids. You have to judge exactly the right moment to give the aids, and you must deliver them very precisely. This takes much practice.

Figures to ride

The top row of figures shows ways of changing the rein – that is, altering the direction in which you are riding round the school. Some of the other figures also involve a change of rein. The aim is to make all these shapes as accurate as possible. A circle should be round, not flattened. A figure-of-eight should be made up of two equal circles. The loops of a serpentine should also be of equal size.

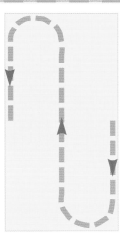

Ride up the centre from the right rein and then turn left to change the rein.

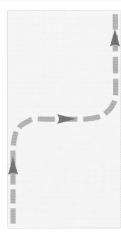

Ride across the centre of the school and then turn left to change the rein.

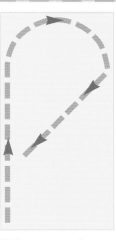

Ride across a short diagonal, such as from M to E, or from corner to corner.

Riding a two-loop serpentine across the centre is another way of changing the rein.

A 5-metre loop is a curve that goes up to 5 metres in from the long side of the school.

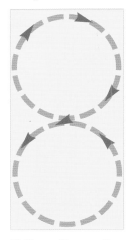

You can ride circles of 10 and 20 metres in diameter from a number of points.

Riding a figure-of-eight's two complete circles involves two changes of rein.

Riding a three-loop serpentine leaves you going in the same direction as you started.

Riding a four-loop serpentine means you end up going round in the opposite direction.

Whole ride no stirrups

When you have riding lessons, you may spend part of each session riding without stirrups. To stop them banging against the pony's sides, you cross them over in front of the saddle. The ride may walk or trot round together, or you may take it in turns to trot round while the rest of the ride walks.

Without stirrups and reins

Once you have had a few riding lessons you may be asked to ride without stirrups, and, later, without reins. Riding without stirrups is an excellent way of improving your seat in the saddle. Riding without reins improves your balance. You should never rely on the reins to keep your balance.

Lungeing without reins

When riding without reins you should tie them in a knot in front of the horse's withers to stop them hanging loose. When you are on a lunge rein, you do not have to worry about steering or stopping the horse, although you will learn to change direction using your legs.

Walk on the lunge
You can concentrate on your position in the saddle and use the leg aids to control the horse's pace and direction.

Trot on the lunge
You may feel insecure when trotting. If so, hold on to the front of the saddle or a neck strap with one or both hands.

Without stirrups

Let your legs hang down beside the pony. Keep them pressed against his sides, with your heels down and your toes up.

Try to sit deep down in the saddle and not bump out of it.

Relax your back so you can follow the pony's movements.

Riding without stirrups is hard work on your muscles, and your legs will ache afterwards.

Holding on to the saddle

When you first ride without stirrups, you will probably hold on to the front of the saddle with one hand while you hold the reins with the other. Your instructor may take you on a leading rein or on the lunge until you become more experienced.

Sit up straight, as if you had stirrups

If you hold both reins in one hand, keep it in the correct position

The instructor will lead your pony very slowly at first to let you get used to being without stirrups

Without reins

Riding without reins is a test of balance. An experienced rider should be able to ride independently of the reins.

Using your leg aids, practise turning the pony right and left.

If you lose your balance, hold the saddle or neck strap.

If your pony misbehaves, or tries to run off, get hold of the reins immediately.

Trot on your own

When you have become more experienced at riding without stirrups you will be allowed to ride on your own. You can walk, trot, canter and even jump without stirrups. You will need to use both hands on the reins, though if you feel unsafe you could rest your hands, still holding the reins, on the front of the saddle. You must keep contact with the pony's mouth.

Forwards and backwards

Keep your seat in the saddle with your legs in the correct position. Then lean forwards to touch the horse's head behind his ears, or as far as you can reach. Go back to your starting position, and then lean backwards to touch the top of the horse's tail, twisting at the waist as you do so. Do not pull on the horse's mouth.

Round the world

In this exercise you go round in a complete circle while sitting on the horse. As you move round, steady yourself by holding on to the saddle.

Exercises in the saddle

Doing stretching and twisting exercises on your pony is good fun. They will help to make you supple, and once you have had a bit of practice doing them, you will become a more confident rider. Start all the exercises by sitting in the correct position in the saddle (see pages 154–155). Only practise the exercises when you have someone with you who can hold your pony.

1 Tie your reins in a knot on the horse's neck and take both your feet out of the stirrups.

2 Lift your right leg over the horse's neck, taking care not to kick him as you do so.

3 Swing your left leg over the quarters. Hold the saddle with your right hand.

4 You are now facing backwards. It feels very odd without the horse's neck in front.

5 Start going back by twisting round and swinging your right leg over the horse's back.

6 Hold on to the front and the back of the saddle as you sit on the horse facing sideways.

7 Shift yourself round in the saddle as you prepare to move your left leg back over again.

8 Swing your left leg back over the horse's neck to return to where you started.

Arm exercises

Stretch your arms high up in the air, then rest your hands on your shoulders. Stretch both your arms out to the sides, and bring your hands back to your shoulders. Reach forwards, and then go back again.

Leg stretching

Sit in the correct position in the saddle and keep the upper part of your legs still. Swing your left leg forwards as far as you can, moving it from the knee downwards. Then swing it back as far as you can. Repeat the exercise with your right leg. Now bring both legs back to the usual position. Moving one at a time, point your feet downwards as far as they will go, then upwards, to stretch your ankles.

Leaning back

You may need to hold on to the front of the saddle to do this exercise, but try to manage without doing so. Simply lean right back until your head is resting on the pony's quarters. Stay there for a moment or two, then sit up again. This is a good way of developing the strong stomach muscles you need for riding.

Touching toes

Lift your right hand up in the air, then bend down over the left side of your saddle and touch your left toe. Straighten up again, and repeat the exercise, lifting your left hand up and bending down to touch your right toe.

Looking forwards

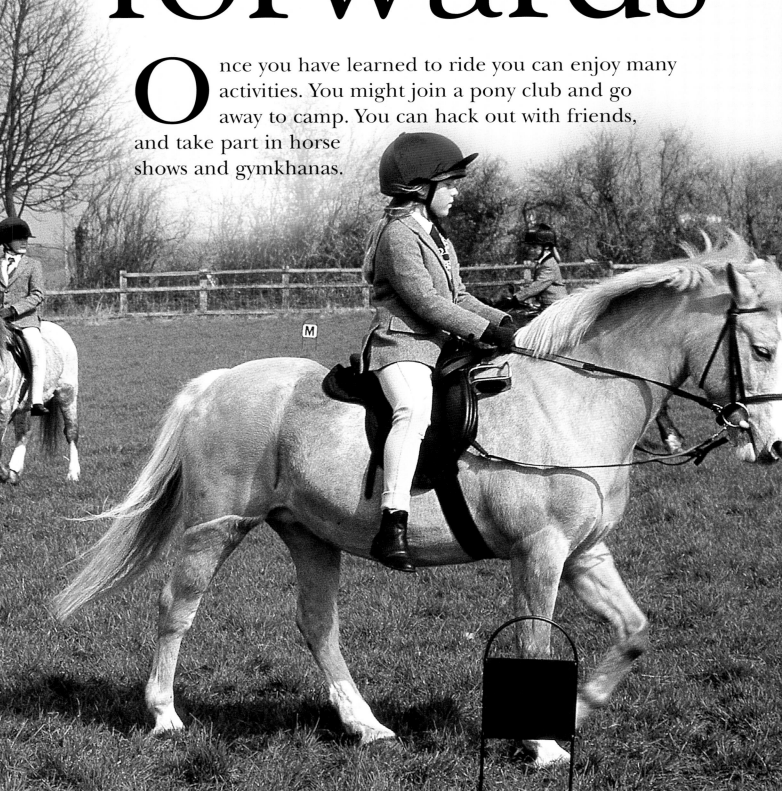

O nce you have learned to ride you can enjoy many activities. You might join a pony club and go away to camp. You can hack out with friends, and take part in horse shows and gymkhanas.

Hand signals on the road

Give clear signals to pedestrians and cyclists as well as drivers, leaving plenty of time before you carry out your intended movement. Hold your reins firmly in the other hand to keep control of your pony.

Turning right
When you wish to turn right, first check behind you that no vehicle is approaching. Hold your right arm out straight to give the signal. Check that it is safe to turn before you do so.

Turning left
To turn left, check for approaching vehicles, then hold your left arm out straight to give the signal. Before you make the turn, check again that it is safe for you to do so.

Riding safely on the road

Always ride on the correct side of the road and keep to the inside. Never ride more than two abreast, and stick to single file on narrow lanes. If you are riding two abreast, then the rider on the inside of a turn to the left or right should make the hand signal.

Road safety

Before you ride out on the road, learn the systems of rules and signals that apply. If possible, take a road safety test. Make sure you can control your pony in all situations. Avoid riding on main roads and narrow roads that do not have grass verges. Never ride on the road at night or when it is foggy.

Thank you
To thank a driver who slows down for you, raise a hand and smile. If you do not wish to take a hand off the reins, nod your head and smile at the driver.

Stop
If you wish to ask another road-user to stop, hold up your right hand in front of you. Do not be afraid of asking drivers to stop or slow down if necessary.

Asking traffic to slow down
To ask a driver to slow down, hold your outside arm out to the side and move it slowly up and down. Thank them when they do slow down.

Light-reflective equipment

You should never ride on a road at night, but on gloomy winter afternoons you can wear light-reflecting safety gear. You can buy reflective belts, tabards and hat covers for yourself, as well as bridle covers, leg bands, tail guards and exercise sheets for your pony. You can also buy lights that clip to your stirrups, showing a white light at the front and red at the back.

Safety tabard
A safety tabard fits over your outdoor clothes. It may have a light-reflective strip across the back and front, or it may feature a warning to other road-users, such as 'Caution: horse and rider', or 'Please pass wide and slow'.

Reflective strip

Safety tabard

Riding out

Hacking – going out for a ride – with friends is fun. If you plan your route beforehand you can make the ride more interesting. You might explore woods and commons – taking in fallen logs as jumps – canter along a bridleway or even ford a shallow stream. Tell an adult where you are going and when you expect to return.

Riding across open ground

It is fun to have a canter or a gallop across open ground if you are allowed to do so, but make sure that you can control your pony before you start. Go uphill if possible, and keep at least a pony's length away from other horses.

Opening and closing gates

A gate on a bridleway should have a catch that you can reach when mounted. You should then be able to open the gate, walk through it and close it without dismounting. Practise at the stables before you try it out riding.

1 Ride right up to the gate and position your pony alongside it so you can reach out to work the catch.

2 Lean forwards to release the catch. Keep your pony standing still with the reins in your other hand.

3 Push the gate open and hold on to it while you ride through. Do not let it swing back on your pony.

4 Once through the gate, turn your pony round and close it again. Make sure the gate is securely shut.

Riding on bridleways

In some areas you may be able to use bridleways – tracks on which horses and ponies are allowed – for all or part of your ride. When riding on a bridleway, follow the signposts and do not stray from the track if it crosses a field. Look out for farm animals, and make sure that any gates you may go through are closed and properly secured.

Riding past other animals

You may ride past a field in which other horses, or cattle, charge about and upset your pony. Try to keep him calm. Keep your reins short and use your legs strongly to ride him past them.

Riding a pony through water

Only cross a stream if you know the water is shallow. Many ponies are nervous of water unless they know that there is firm ground beneath it. Let the pony take his time at first, but then drive him on firmly with your legs and seat.

Your first jumping lessons

Approach
The approach to a jump is all-important. You must drive the pony firmly forwards with pressure from your legs.

Learning to jump is very exciting. There is much to learn, but if you ride correctly over trotting poles and small fences, in time big fences will not be a problem. The pony must be moving with impulsion before take-off, and you must follow his movement over the jump.

Forward position

For jumping or galloping you need to learn forward position. When jumping, shorten the stirrups a hole or two. Lift your bottom clear of the saddle and lean forwards, taking your weight on your knees and on your feet in the stirrups.

Leading over poles

First jumping lessons for both ponies and riders are usually over poles laid on the ground and spaced so the pony can walk and trot over them. To start with, your instructor may lead your pony over them.

The galloping position

You also use forward position when galloping to take the weight off the horse's back. Shorten your reins and keep your knees pressed into the saddle and your heels down. If your heels come up you will lose your balance.

1 As you approach the poles, shorten your reins slightly and go into forward position. Drive the pony on with your legs. Keep your heels down and your head up, and look ahead to where you are going.

2 The pony will lift up his feet to trot over the poles. He should move smoothly and evenly, with a regular rhythm, and not jump over the poles. Use rising trot when you are trotting over poles.

Keep your legs in contact with the pony's sides and your heels down during the jump. Feel the reins, but do not pull.

Take-off
When the pony's hind legs propel him into the air, lean forwards to go with his movement. Let your hands follow his head.

Trotting pole practice

Trotting over poles is a good exercise for a pony. Lay three or four poles 1 to 1.3m apart, according to the pony's size. When the spacing is correct, the pony's hind foot will hit the ground mid-way between two of the poles.

1 Walk over the poles at first. Go round the school and try approaching them from both directions. Use forward position as you ride over the poles.

2 When you are happy in walk, trot round the school and, as you go round, take in the row of poles. Keep a good rhythm in the trot, and look ahead as you ride, not at the poles.

Your first jump

After trotting poles, you will learn to take your first jump. It will not be very high. Crossed poles encourage the pony to jump in the centre, where the fence is lower. Wings placed at each side of a jump help to prevent the pony from avoiding it and running out. This counts as a refusal in competitions.

Landing
When the pony lands, keep the forward position and take care you do not pull on his mouth.

Sequence of a jump

A jump can be divided into four parts: the approach, the take-off, in the air and landing. You can approach a jump in trot or canter – both must be balanced and rhythmical. The take-off must be at the right distance if the horse is to clear the fence. Once he has landed, do not hesitate but ride him straight on towards the next fence.

Getting larger

Once you are confident jumping a low rail, you can try something a bit more ambitious. Keeping fences quite low, but making them wider is a good way to progress. Your pony will have to stretch out further to clear them.

Top-class jumping

To clear huge fences like this (right), the horse has to stretch his head and neck right out. Only a few horses and riders reach this top level. This is Sheila Burke on Genius 79 in the USA in 1998.

Jumping higher

If you want to do really well at showjumping, you need to spend a lot of time schooling your pony. You will need to train on the flat as well as practise over fences. Flat work is important because to jump well your pony needs to be supple and obedient. He must listen to your commands so he does not rush his fences or take off at the wrong moment. When you are jumping, whether for practice or in the ring, you should drive your pony forwards with your seat and legs so that he knows for certain what you want from him.

Seeing a stride

Three or four strides before a fence, try to judge how many strides your pony should take before he takes off. This is called 'seeing a stride'. If a pony gets too near a fence, he will not be able to jump it. If he is too far away, he may knock a pole with his hindlegs.

Water jump

Maria Gretzer (above) rides Feliciano over a water jump at Hickstead, England in 1999. A water jump is a wide pool with a low fence on the take-off side. The horse has to stretch out to jump the obstacle without putting a foot in the water.

Double combination

Four-fence combination

Combination

Two or more fences close together count as one obstacle, called a combination. If a horse refuses at one part, he has to jump the whole sequence again. The number of strides between fences in a combination can vary.

Schooling steps

Once you have learned to control your pony and are confident doing basic work in the school, you may progress to more advanced schooling and simple dressage movements. Even if you do not go on to enter any competitions, careful schooling will help you to learn to communicate with your horse or pony and get the most from him.

On the bit

When your pony is working properly it is said to be 'on the bit'. The pony will hold its head vertically, with the mouth lower than your hands. With your pony in this position, you will have maximum control with only a light feel on the reins.

Square halt

With practice, a rider can stop a horse so that he is standing square. This means his forefeet and hindfeet are in line with each other. He must stay in balance throughout the halt.

Turning on the forehand

The horse's hindlegs move round his inside foreleg. To turn to the right, feel the right rein, bring the left rein over in support, press with your left leg and hold the quarters steady with your right leg.

Shoulder-in
The horse's forelegs follow an inner track. He crosses his forelegs as he travels but his hindlegs move straight forwards.

Lateral work

Lateral means 'sideways'. In lateral work, the horse's body forms a curve, so his forelegs move on a different track from his hindlegs. For this reason, lateral work is also known as 'work on two tracks'.

Travers
The horse's hindlegs follow an inner track. His body is bent to the outside of the school.

Leg yield
The horse moves forwards and sideways away from his rider's leg. His body is straight.

Riding side-saddle

To ride side-saddle, you face the front, with your right leg over a pommel called the 'fixed head'. Your left leg rests under another pommel – the leaping head. It is supported by a single stirrup. The saddle is secured by a girth and a balance strap. A pony has special training to carry a side-saddle, and responds to a whip on the right side instead of the rider's leg.

Counter canter

Horses and ponies normally lead with their inside leg when they canter, but for a movement called the counter canter, they need to lead with their outside leg. This is difficult to perform, and the horse needs to be well balanced.

Advanced riding

If you watch a top-class dressage partnership, the horse seems to carry out perfect movements effortlessly, and the rider appears to give no visible aids. It will be a long time before you can carry out advanced dressage paces and movements properly. But remember, even the best riders were not born champions. They have spent many years working hard and patiently.

The art of riding

The classical art of riding is practised by the Spanish Riding School of Vienna in Austria and the Cadre Noir of Saumur in France. Riders at these schools perform complicated steps based on the horse's natural movements. This horse is performing a levade – a controlled half-rear.

Spanish School

Turn on the haunches

This is when a horse pivots round his inside hindleg, which should remain still. He uses his other legs in the same sequence as he would when going forwards.

Collection and extension

Collection is a shortening of the horse's outline. His stride is shorter and more elevated, and the pace is slower. Extension is the opposite. The horse stretches out his head and neck, and he takes longer, lower strides, which increase his speed.

Collected to extended walk
As the horse moves from a collected walk, through medium walk into an extended walk, he gradually lengthens his stride and stretches out his head and neck.

Collected walk

Collected trot
The horse moves at a steady, collected pace, but still with energy. His head and neck are raised and his hindquarters appear lower.

R

Extended trot
Here, the horse is moving faster, with a longer stride. As he extends the trot, he flicks his front feet forwards.

Flying change

When a horse changes the leading leg at canter, while all his feet are off the ground, it is called a 'flying change'. It is a difficult movement to perform. An experienced horse and rider may do a flying change every stride.

Half-pass

This is a lateral movement in which the horse moves forwards and sideways at the same time. He crosses his outside legs over in front of the inside legs, bending his head in the direction in which he is going. This horse (right) is moving to the left.

In the air
This horse has changed legs in the air, and is now leading with his right leg.

Collected/medium walk

Medium walk

Extended walk

Free walk on a long rein

Collected canter
The collected canter is a slow, rocking pace. The horse must be supple and relaxed. The rider should sit deep in the saddle and follow the movement.

Extended canter
The horse stretches his neck and lengthens his stride to cover as much ground as possible. Both horse and rider's centres of gravity move forwards.

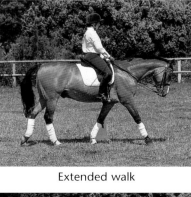

Taking part in
events

You may enjoy simply riding your pony around the countryside, but if you want to compete, there are all kinds of activities in which you can take part. You may want to join a riding club or go on sponsored rides. You can enter showing, jumping and gymkhana competitions at local shows, and you might like to try dressage or hunter trials.

Riding clubs
Local riding clubs hold all sorts of events. If you become a member you can take part, and also find out about other equestrian activities going on in your area.

Endurance riding
If you take part in a long-distance endurance ride, you and your pony will need to be very fit. You may have to cover up to 80km a day. Arab horses have good stamina and excel at this sport.

Vaulting
Vaulting is gymnastics on horseback, and requires great athletic ability as well as riding skills. You can take part on your own or as part of a team, performing leaps and balancing feats with the horse on a lunge rein.

Plaiting the mane

1 Dampen the mane. Start at the top of the neck and divide it into equal bunches. Secure each bunch with an elastic band until you plait it.

2 Plait each bunch tightly and neatly and secure it with an elastic band at the end. Thread a needle with cotton that matches the mane.

3 Tie a large knot in the end of the cotton and sew through the end of the plait. Loop the plait under and sew it firmly in place.

4 Loop the plait in half again and sew it up, catching in any stray hairs. Finish with a knot close to the underside of the plait and cut the cotton.

Getting ready for the show

Getting ready for a show is great fun, but it takes a lot of time and hard work to do it properly. You may need to give your pony a bath, if the weather is warm enough, otherwise you can just groom him thoroughly. You will need to wash his mane and tail before plaiting them. You can also oil his hooves and make sure his tack is really clean so that he will look his best.

Bands or sewn?
You can secure your pony's plaits with elastic bands, but if you are entering a showing class or competing in dressage, you must sew them in place.

Making the most of your pony

Quarter marks

Make quarter marks on your pony's hindquarters by wetting the coat and brushing it at different angles. You can also use special stencils to make squares or diamonds. Use hair spray to make the marks last longer.

Trim hairy fetlocks and any coarse hairs under the jaw.

Make white tails and markings extra white by rubbing in chalk.

Oil the hooves when they are clean, to make them look smart.

Pulling a mane

Pull a mane to tidy it up before you plait it. Use a pulling comb to separate a few long hairs at a time from underneath, then pull.

Hairdressing
If you end up with a few wisps of hair sticking out of the plaits, put some hair gel on them and smooth them down flat.

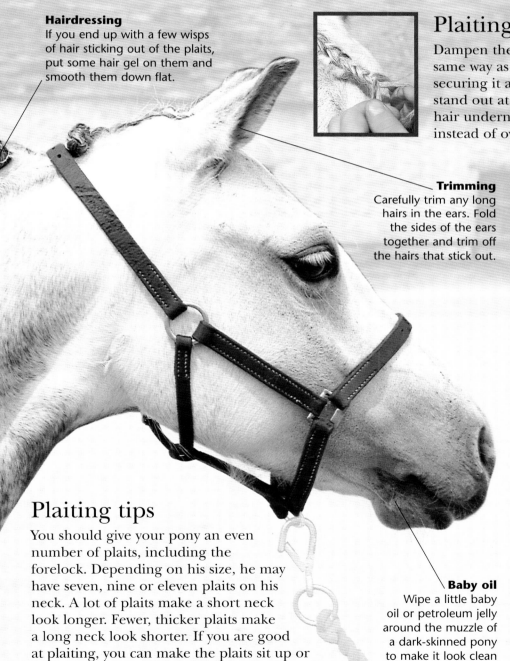

Plaiting the forelock

Dampen the forelock and plait it in the same way as the mane, sewing it and securing it as before. To make the plait stand out at the top, cross the strands of hair underneath as you are plaiting, instead of over the top.

Trimming
Carefully trim any long hairs in the ears. Fold the sides of the ears together and trim off the hairs that stick out.

Plaiting tips

You should give your pony an even number of plaits, including the forelock. Depending on his size, he may have seven, nine or eleven plaits on his neck. A lot of plaits make a short neck look longer. Fewer, thicker plaits make a long neck look shorter. If you are good at plaiting, you can make the plaits sit up or lie flat to make the neck look wider or narrower.

Baby oil
Wipe a little baby oil or petroleum jelly around the muzzle of a dark-skinned pony to make it look clean and shiny.

Plaiting the tail

Plait an unpulled tail for neatness. Take long hairs from each side of the dock and plait them with hair from the centre. Gradually take in more hair from the sides as you work down the tail. Secure the end, fold it under and sew it in place.

Going to a show

Competing in a show is great fun. After all the preparation, it is exciting to ride round the ring, looking your best and trying your hardest. In between classes, do not tear around, but let your pony rest in the shade. Give him a drink and some hay or grazing. It is great to win a rosette, but do not blame your pony or get upset if you fail to do so. There is always next time.

Unloading backwards
If your pony needs to back out of a trailer, stand at his head and push him gently backwards. Ask someone to stand by the ramp to guide him.

Unloading safely

Untie your pony before you take down the breastbar or rear strap. Lead him out forwards if you can. When you go down the ramp, do not let him rush. Some ramps are slippery and quite steep, and he could hurt himself if he goes too fast. Ask two friends to stand on either side of the ramp if you think he might try to jump off sideways.

Unloading forwards
If the box or trailer has a side ramp, you can lead your pony out forwards. Do not let him pull you out. Walk down calmly.

First things first
Tie up your pony or ask someone to hold him while you take off his boots. Check him all over to see that he is all right after the journey.

Ready to jump
If you are entering a jumping event, you must wear a body protector that meets the safety standards.

Ready to show
Look as smart as you can for a showing class. It will give you confidence if you look your best.

Waiting safely

Leave your pony tied to a trailer only if you know he will not get upset. Fasten his lead rope to a piece of string so he can break free if he panics. Your pony will probably wait patiently if you hang up some hay for him.

The secretary

When you arrive at the showground, check in at the show secretary's tent or trailer. You can collect your number here and enter classes if you have not already done so. You can also find the results of classes here. The secretary will post them up on a noticeboard.

Sharing a pony

If you are sharing a pony with a friend, make sure you agree in advance which classes you will enter. It is fun to watch each other and help prepare for the classes. But do not ask your pony to do too much and exhaust him.

Fun and games

At gymkhanas and shows there are all kinds of games and races for you to try. Some are for teams, and some for individuals. You need to be good at games, able to think and act quickly, and to have an obedient and fast-moving pony. If you belong to a pony club you could become a member of the team and compete around the country.

Flag relay
This is a team game in which you have to gallop to a flag, lean over and pick it up, then gallop back and hand it on to the next member of your team.

Handy tips

You need to be quick-witted, fit and athletic to do really well in mounted games.

Your pony must be fast, agile, and above all, obedient – it is no use asking him to gallop if you cannot get him to stop or turn.

Barrel racing
A pony that can gallop and turn quickly without losing his balance is a great help in this race round barrels.

Practice makes perfect

No matter what games you enter, you need to practise for them. Schooling your pony until he is obedient to all your commands will make a big difference on the day. Practise going from halt to canter to gallop, and changing pace and direction at speed. See how quickly you can mount and dismount, and learn how to vault on and off. You can also get used to leaning out of the saddle to pick up things.

Vaulting on

Being able to vault on to your pony while he is moving saves a lot of time in games and races. It is easier if your pony is small and you have long legs! You have to run with him, holding the saddle, then spring up and swing yourself over.

Egg and spoon
You need a steady hand for this. The eggs are not real, but you still have to keep one on the spoon!

Tyre race
You and a partner have to leap off your ponies, climb through a tyre and then get back on again.

Make a tower
You have to lean right out of the saddle to stack the plastic tubs without overbalancing in this race.

Potato race
Having picked up a potato and raced down the field, you then have to throw it into a bucket.

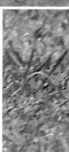

Showjumping classes

Showjumping is a popular riding sport. All classes have a time limit, but some are against the clock, where the fastest clear round wins. You are penalized for knocking down a fence, refusing, running out (going round the side of a fence) and falling. Three refusals or taking the wrong course means elimination. If more than one person jumps a clear round, there is a 'jump off'. This means you have to ride a shorter course to decide the winner.

Triple bars
Three bars making a wide spread

Brush and rails
A spread highest in the centre

Gate
A high, upright fence

Wall
Made of 'bricks' that fall off easily

Filler
A solid part below the poles

Upright poles
Poles straight above each other

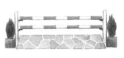

Double oxer
Brush between two sets of poles

Hog's back
The highest pole is in the centre

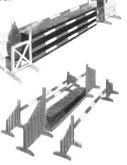

Walking the course

Before a showjumping class, all the competitors have a chance to walk the course. This gives you time to plan and memorize the route you will take. You can also look carefully at each jump, and judge how many strides your pony will need to take between the parts of the combination fences.

In the collecting ring

The collecting ring is an area, usually with one or two practice jumps, where you can warm up your pony before his class. Once the class has started, you will have to wait near the entrance to the ring for your number to be called.

Types of jump

Show jumps fall into four main categories: uprights, spreads, combinations and water. Uprights are difficult for ponies to jump. Spread fences are easier because they are lower at the front. Combinations – jumps with only a stride or two between each fence – need good judgment from pony and rider. To clear water jumps, ponies have to stretch themselves out.

Thinking ahead

Throughout your round, it is important to keep a good position in the saddle. Urge your pony forwards confidently as you jump, and look ahead to the next fence.

Saving time

It is important to memorize the course before you enter the ring so that, as you land from each jump, you can be thinking about the next one. Against the clock, you can save precious seconds by taking the shortest route between fences.

Clear round

Do not tear around the ring – your pony will lose balance and hit fences.

Drive him firmly towards each fence. If he feels you hesitate, he is likely to refuse.

If you feel he may refuse, a sharp tap with your stick behind the girth may work.

Do not hit your pony if he knocks a fence – just try to approach it better next time.

Showing and dressage tests

To compete in the show ring and dressage arena you need a well-schooled horse or pony, and both of you must be clean and smart. In the show ring, a pony is judged on his conformation (his shape and proportions), his paces and his behaviour. You will have to ride at walk and trot, and canter on both reins; walk and trot your pony in hand; and sometimes do an individual show.

Showing in hand

When you are lined up in the ring, you will be asked to take off your pony's saddle so that the judge can inspect him. Then you will have to walk and trot him in hand so the judge can check that he moves straight.

Individual show

An individual show is a chance to show off your pony's paces. Most people ride circles at trot and canter on both reins, or combine them to form a figure-of-eight. At the end of your time, finish with a good square halt.

Before the test

Before doing a dressage test, ride in a pony thoroughly to get him settled and working at his best. Some horses and ponies need more work than others, so give yourself plenty of time.

Riding the test

Concentrate and keep calm when riding in the dressage arena. The judges who mark the test write their comments on a score sheet. You will be given the sheet, and it is a useful pointer to your strengths and weaknesses.

Dressage hints and tips

Check that your clothes and tack meet the requirements of the competition.

Make sure that you and your pony are immaculately clean and well-groomed. It is important to make a good first impression on the judges.

Ask someone to call out each bit of the test as you practise, to help you to remember it.

Make up rhymes to help you memorize the test.

Practise until you and your pony can carry out the test's requirements perfectly.

Aim for the top

Some riders and their horses specialize in dressage. Isabell Werth and Nissan Gigolo are doing an extended trot at the World Equestrian Games in 1998. A great deal of training lies behind the tests performed by top-class horses and riders.

Hedge

Ski jump

Log

Tyres

Rails

Cross-country

On a cross-country course, there are solid fences with long spaces in between. Both you and your pony need to be strong and brave. You will pick up penalty points for every mistake you make, such as refusing, jumping the wrong part of a fence, going the wrong way, falling off or going over the time limit. The fences carry red and white flags. You must jump between them with the red on your right and the white on your left. You may have the choice between an easier, slower route or a faster, more difficult one.

Types of fence

Cross-country fences are based on obstacles you might meet if you were riding through the countryside, such as rails, hedges, logs, walls, ditches, banks and water. They are solid and do not give way if hit. They may be placed so that you have to jump them going up, or down, hills.

Hunter trials

Cross-country jumping competitions are called hunter trials. There are trials for both horses and ponies. Courses often take you through fields and woodland, and you may have to open and close a gate. There is usually a set time in which you must try to finish one section or the whole course.

Walking the course

You are allowed to walk round a cross-country course before you ride it. This allows you to look at the fences and work out the best way to approach them. Check the ground on the approach and landing, and look out for things that might spook your pony, so that you are prepared.

Horse trials

In horse trials, you have to do dressage, cross-country and showjumping. These are the supreme test of horse and rider. Precision and training is needed for the dressage; endurance, speed and boldness for the cross-country; and suppleness and obedience for the showjumping. Experienced riders take part in events that last for two or three days. This is Andrew Nicholson and New York, at a three-day event.

Steeplechase

Two- and three-day events include a steeplechase phase – about 12 fences over a distance of about 3.6km. The course has to be ridden at around 41km/h, which means a horse has to perform like a racehorse. At large events, competitors also have to ride along sections of roads and tracks, both before and after the steeplechase.

Training & driving

Breaking to harness

When the horse or pony has got used to wearing harness and being long-reined, the traces can be attached to an old tyre to get him used to dragging something behind him. The trainer walks behind holding the long reins.

Long-reining off the bit

In this advanced form of long-reining, the reins are attached to the horse's bit and pass through rings on the roller. The outside rein passes round the horse's quarters.

A horse's or pony's training begins when he is a very young foal. If he is handled with kindness, firmness, patience and understanding, he will grow up to be confident, and he will learn to trust people. This trust forms the basis for all his education. When he is three or four years old, his training will become more specialized, depending on whether he is to be ridden, driven, or both. A few horses, through careful, patient teaching and much practice, go on to become stars in their own specialist area, whether it be dressage, show-jumping, eventing, police work, pulling a ceremonial carriage or carrying a military bandsman.

Breaking in a horse

Teaching a horse or pony to accept a rider and to understand the rider's signals, or 'aids', is called 'breaking it in'. The horse has to learn to wear a saddle and bridle, and to have a bit in his mouth. Lungeing and long-reining help strengthen his muscles and make him supple.

Lunge cavesson and rein

A lunge cavesson has a padded noseband fitted with three rings which are set on swivels.

Lungeing with side reins

Side reins, running from a snaffle bit to a roller, help adjust the horse's balance so he carries himself as if he had a rider. They also encourage him to make contact with the bit.

Lungeing with saddle

Once the horse has got used to the feel of a saddle on his back, he can be lunged wearing it, with the side reins in place. It is another step forwards in his education.

Lungeing a horse

When being lunged, a horse moves at a walk, trot and canter in a circle round the trainer. At first, an assistant leads the horse, but later he obeys his trainer's words of command.

Long-reining with side reins

Long-reining teaches the horse to change direction and pace by means of the reins. He also learns how to balance and carry himself without the complication of the rider's weight.

Halter breaking

A foal is trained to wear a headcollar and be led beside its mother when it is a few days old. Once it gets used to being led, one person can manage both mare and foal.

Backing a young horse

Before sitting in the saddle for the first time, the rider leans across it, to accustom the horse to her weight.

First lessons

Once in the saddle, without stirrups in case she needs to dismount quickly, the rider sits very quietly on the horse while the trainer leads it round the school.

Using a saddle

An alternative method of long-reining is to use a saddle and pass the reins through the stirrup irons, with the leathers shortened so the irons do not bang against the horse's sides.

How to drive a horse

When you are driving, you control a horse or pony by means of your voice, the reins and the whip. 'Walk on' and 'trot on', said in an encouraging tone, tell the horse to move forwards. 'Whoa', said more slowly and reinforced with the reins, tell it to slow down or stop. A properly trained horse obeys the lightest of touches and commands.

Putting to

'Putting to' means attaching the vehicle to the horse's harness. The reins are looped over the horse's back. One person holds the horse while another brings up the vehicle and hooks the traces on to the trace hooks.

Fastening a tug

Tugs are leather loops through which the ends of the shafts pass. They are buckled to the back band which passes over the saddle. By holding the shafts steady, tugs prevent the vehicle tipping up or down.

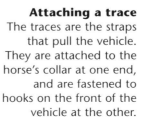

Fastening a breeching strap
The breeching straps pass through metal staples on the shafts called the breeching dees, and fasten round the shafts and the traces.

Attaching a trace
The traces are the straps that pull the vehicle. They are attached to the horse's collar at one end, and are fastened to hooks on the front of the vehicle at the other.

Scurry driving

Scurry driving is a type of speed-driving competition in which small ponies such as Shetlands excel. Contestants are timed as they drive round an obstacle course, often leaning at alarming angles as they go round corners.

Holding reins and whip

Your left hand holds both reins, as shown here, with the left rein uppermost. Your right hand holds the whip.

Turning

If they hold the reins as shown above (left rein between the thumb and forefinger; right rein between the second and third fingers) an experienced person can turn a driven horse to the right by turning their left hand so its palm faces upwards. This puts more tension on the right rein and less on the left. To turn left, the palm of the hand faces downwards, tensioning the left rein and releasing the right rein.

Turning left
When you are learning to drive, or if you need a stronger aid, your right hand can reinforce the pressure on the left rein, holding it just in front of the left hand.

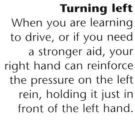

Turning right
To give a stronger aid for turning right, you use your right hand to put direct pressure on the right rein. Your right hand should not move too far away from your left hand.

Using the whip

When driving, your voice and the whip tell the horse to move forwards. The whip should just touch him lightly between the collar and the saddle.

Harness and vehicles

Harness and vehicles vary according to the purpose for which they are used. A pony pulling a fast, lightweight vehicle such as a gig wears lighter harness than a horse drawing a heavy coach. The harness may use either a neck collar or a breast collar, and may be ornamented with metal fittings. Horses and ponies are usually harnessed singly, in twos (side by side as a pair, or one behind the other as a tandem) or in fours.

Browband
This elegant show bridle has a brass-mounted browband.

Rosette
This is a metal boss at the end of the browband which sometimes bears the owner's crest or monogram.

Saddle
The padded driving saddle protects the pony's back from the weight of the vehicle which is carried there.

Trace
The traces pull the vehicle.

Hames
Hames are metal arms that fit round the collar, to which the traces are attached.

Collar
Through the collar, the pony takes the vehicle's weight on his shoulders.

Girth
The girth holds the saddle firmly in place.

Driving bridle and Liverpool bit

A driving bridle usually has blinkers to prevent the horse seeing, and being frightened by, the vehicle behind it. The Liverpool bit (left) has three rein positions. The top, on the ring, is the mildest, the bottom the most severe.

Trandem

A team of three horses harnessed abreast is called a trandem, and is rarely seen. The horses shown here are Shires.

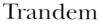

Reins
The reins pass through terrets (rings) on the hames and saddle.

Breeching
The breeching, which is attached to the shafts, allows the pony to stop the vehicle.

Stick-back gig

In the 19th century, gigs were a popular form of transport. Nowadays they are often used by private driving enthusiasts. Lightweight and elegant, they can be drawn by a single pony or a pair.

Royal coach

This splendid ceremonial coach, seen here at the Royal Windsor Horse Show in England, is owned by Queen Elizabeth II. The horses' harness and the men's livery are richly decorated.

Specially trained horses

Police horses, and those used for military ceremonies, undergo special training after they have been broken in. London police horses start between the ages of five and seven years. Each spends six months 'at school', learning not to be afraid of loud noises, waving flags and unruly crowds. This is followed by six months on patrol with an experienced horse. Horses used by the Household Cavalry follow a similar regime.

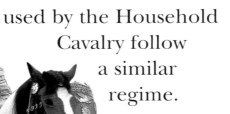

Drum horse

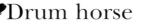

Drum horses are always heavy horses, as they must carry a rider plus the two drums, which weigh over 27kg each. The drummer controls his horse with foot reins.

Police horses in America

Controlling crowds in city centres is everyday work for police horses all round the world. In many places, including Britain, horses doing similar work wear protective guards over their eyes and heads.

King's Troop Royal Horse Artillery

The King's Troop Royal Horse Artillery carries out ceremonial duties in Britain, such as firing royal salutes and providing gun carriages and black horses for state funerals. They are famous for their Musical Drive, the climax of which is the amazing 'scissor' movement, in which teams of galloping horses drawing gun carriages cross in the centre of the arena with split-second timing.

Parade duty

Part of a London police horse's duties is to escort military bands in ceremonial parades. An untrained horse would be upset by the noise; the police horse is calm and unruffled.

Ring of fire

Jumping through a flaming hoop is one of the most spectacular parts of a police horse display. The horses are first trained to jump the box alone, then they jump the box through the hoop. Next, just part of the hoop is lit. An experienced horse gives a lead.

Glossary

The horse and pony world has a language of its own, and you might not understand all the words you read and hear. This list explains what some of these words mean.

action The way a horse or pony moves.

aids The signals that a rider uses to tell a horse what to do. Natural aids are the rider's legs, **seat**, **hands** and voice. Artificial aids include whips and spurs.

American barn A kind of stabling in which a large barn is divided into several **loose boxes** on either side of a central aisle.

approach The last few **strides** a horse or pony takes before a jump.

backing Getting on a horse for the first time.

balance A horse is balanced when his weight, and that of his rider, is distributed in such a way that he can move easily and efficiently.

bit The part of a bridle that goes in a horse's mouth – usually made of steel.

blaze A white mark down the front of a horse's face.

body brush A short-bristled brush used for removing dirt and grease from a horse's or pony's coat.

body protector A rigid waistcoat that helps to protect your back from injury if you fall off a horse or pony.

bone The measurement round the **cannon bone**, just below the **knee**. 'Plenty of bone' means a high measurement and therefore strong legs.

bounce fence A combination fence with no stride between the two elements. A horse lands from one and immediately takes off again for the other.

breastplate A strap that goes round a horse's neck and fastens to the front of the saddle and to the girth. It prevents the saddle from slipping backwards.

breeching Part of driving harness that helps the horse stop the vehicle it is pulling.

breeching strap a) The strap that attaches the **breeching** to the shafts. b) A strap which is fastened across the back of a trailer to stop a horse from moving backwards.

breed society An organization that regulates the breeding of its particular breed of horse or pony.

bridoon A **snaffle bit** used with a **double bridle**.

browband The part of a bridle that fits round a horse's or pony's forehead and stops the **headpiece** from slipping backwards.

bucking A horse kicking out its back legs with its head down, or jumping in the air with all four feet off the ground and the back arched.

cannon bone The bone in the foreleg between the **knee** and the **fetlock**.

cantle The back of a saddle.

cavesson a) A type of **noseband**. b) A headcollar with swivel rings to which a lunge rein is attached.

chaff Chopped hay and straw, which is mixed with other feed to stop horses eating it too quickly.

changing the rein Changing the direction in which you are riding in the **school** or show ring.

chaps Leather or suede over-trousers to protect a rider's legs when riding. They may be full-length, or half-chaps up to the knee.

cheeks a) The flat sides of a horse's face. b) The vertical side parts of a **curb bit**.

cheekpiece The part of a bridle that supports the **bit**.

cinch The **girth** on a Western saddle.

clean-legged Legs that carry no **feather**.

clenches The ends of horseshoe nails that are hammered down to hold the shoe in place.

clipping Removing a horse's or pony's winter coat to enable it to work without sweating excessively.

coarse mix A type of prepared **hard feed** in which various ingredients are mixed together.

cob A short-legged, small, stocky horse, usually with a **quiet temperament**. The mane is often hogged.

colic Abdominal pain. Colic can be very serious and needs veterinary attention.

collar Part of driving **harness** which rests on the horse's shoulders.

collection Moving with shorter, more elevated **strides**, thus shortening the horse's or pony's **outline**.

colt A male horse under the age of four years.

competition horse A horse that takes part in competitions, usually **eventing**, **dressage** or showjumping.

concentrates The grains such as oats and barley that make up **hard feed**.

conformation The overall shape and proportions of a horse or pony.

contact The link through the **reins** between a horse's mouth and his rider's **hands**.

crest The centre of the arch on the **top line** of the neck.

cross-country A riding course with jumps which must be completed within a specified time. Cross-country is part of **eventing**.

croup The highest point of the hindquarters.

curb bit A bit with **cheeks** and a curb chain that acts on a horse's head and chin as well as his mouth.

curry comb a) A metal comb on a wooden handle used for cleaning a **body brush**. b) A plastic or rubber version that can be used on a horse or pony to remove mud and loose hairs from its coat.

dandy brush A wooden-backed brush with long, stiff bristles used for removing dried mud and for grooming a field-kept pony.

deep litter A system of stable management in which only the droppings are removed in daily mucking out, and fresh bedding is placed on top of the old.

deep through the girth Deep and broad through the chest and behind the elbows. This gives lots of space for the heart and lungs.

diagonal a) A pair of the horse's legs diagonally opposite each other, e.g. left fore, right hind. b) A slanting line across a **school**.

dished face A face that is concave, or curving inwards, like the Arab's.

dishing A horse moving by throwing his front feet out to the sides instead of going straight; a fault in his action.

disunited Cantering with one leg leading in front and the opposite leg leading behind.

DIY livery A way of keeping a horse at a **livery** stable where the owner visits each day and does all the work.

dock The area under the top of a horse's tail, and the top part of the tail itself.

double bridle A type of bridle with two **bits**.

draught horse A big, heavy horse used for pulling loads or farm implements.

dressage The advanced **schooling** and training of a horse, performed in competitions.

dropped noseband A **noseband** that fastens under the **bit**, preventing a horse from opening his mouth to avoid the action of the bit.

eel stripe A dark stripe along a horse's or pony's back, from its mane to its tail. Seen on Asiatic breeds, and Fjord and Highland ponies.

eventing A competition comprising **dressage**, **cross-country** and **showjumping**.

extension Moving with longer, lower **strides**, thus lengthening the horse's or pony's **outline**.

feather The long hair that grows on the lower part of the legs of most heavy horses and some ponies.

fender A leather flap that covers the stirrup leather on a Western saddle.

fetlock The joint on the lower part of a horse's leg just above the foot.

field shelter An open-fronted shed in a field that provides horses and ponies with some protection from the weather.

filly A female horse under the age of four years.

flat work **Schooling** 'on the ground', not over fences.

flying change Changing the **leading leg** at canter when a horse has all four feet off the ground.

foal A horse or pony under the age of one year.

forage Food for a horse or pony, especially grass, hay and **haylage**.

forehand The head, neck, shoulders, **withers** and forelegs of a horse or pony.

forelock The part of a horse's or pony's mane that falls over his forehead.

forward position Leaning forwards with the seat off the saddle, taking the weight on the knees and feet, used when galloping and jumping.

four-beat pace One in which each foot hits the ground separately, such as the walk.

frog The V-shaped structure in the sole of a horse's foot.

full livery Keeping a horse or pony at a **livery** stable where the stable staff carry out all the work involved.

gait The **pace** at which a horse or pony moves. The natural gaits are walk, trot, canter and gallop.

gaited An American term describing a horse that can perform more gaits than the natural ones. Horses may be three-gaited or five-gaited.

gamgee Cotton wool lined with gauze, used as a padding under leg bandages.

gelding A castrated male horse or pony – one not able to breed.

gig A lightweight, two-wheeled, horse-drawn vehicle seating two people.

girth The broad strap that goes round a horse's belly to hold the saddle in place.

going The condition of the ground for riding: wet ground is described as soft or heavy going; dry ground is described as hard going.

grass livery Keeping a horse or pony out at grass at a **livery** stable.

grazing rotation Grazing a field with cattle and sheep after horses to even out the pasture and prevent the build-up of worm eggs.

gymkhana Mounted games and races, usually performed as part of a show.

hack a) To go out for a ride. b) A type of horse suitable for riding.

hackamore A type of bitless bridle.

half-bred A horse or pony with one **Thoroughbred** parent.

hands a) The units used to measure a horse's height. One hand equals 10cm. b) A rider who has light, yet positive, control of the **reins** is said to have good hands.

hard feed Corn, pony nuts, **coarse mixes** and so on, fed to a horse in small quantities.

harness The equipment used on a horse that is being driven. 'In harness' means being driven.

haylage Vacuum-packed, partly dried hay. It is dust-free and fed to horses with breathing problems.

headpiece The part of a bridle or headcollar that goes over the horse's head.

hh Stands for 'hands high'.

hogging Cutting off a horse's or pony's mane.

horse An equine animal which stands 14.3 **hands** (150cm) high or taller.

hunter A horse used for hunting. It must be able to gallop and jump well.

hunting cap A velvet-covered hard riding hat which has a brim.

impulsion The energy a rider creates in a horse by the use of the legs and **seat**.

in hand Leading a horse or pony while on foot.

inbred Bred from animals that are closely related to each other.

jog a) A slow trot. b) A **pace** in Western riding.

jump off An extra round or rounds, used to decide the winner in **showjumping** when two or more competitors have the same score.

keeper A small loop on a strap through which the end is put to keep it flat and tidy.

knee The joint halfway down the foreleg.

laminitis A painful inflammation of the inside of a horse's feet, usually caused by over-feeding.

landing The stage of a jump when the horse's feet reach the ground again.

lateral At the side. A lateral **pace** is when both legs on the same side move together.

leading file The horse and rider at the front of a group.

leading leg The leg that is in advance of the others when a horse is cantering.

leg into hand A riding term meaning that you create energy in the horse or pony with your legs and control it with your **hands**.

leg up An easy way of getting on a horse. A helper holds the rider's left leg and helps him or her to spring up into the saddle.

Liverpool bit A driving bit with three different rein positions.

livery Keeping a horse or pony on someone else's premises, and paying them to look after it for you.

loading Putting a horse into a horsebox or trailer.

long-reining Driving a horse while on foot.

loose box A stable in which a horse is free to move about.

lungeing Exercising a horse on a long rein attached to a special headcollar. The horse is asked to walk, trot and canter in circles.

manège An enclosed arena used for riding and schooling.

mare A female horse or pony aged four years or more.

markings, record of A horse's or pony's markings are recorded on vaccination certificates and passports.

martingale A piece of **tack** designed to stop a horse from throwing its head up too high. A standing martingale runs from the **noseband** to the **girth**; a running martingale from the **reins** to the girth.

mealy Light-coloured, the colour of oatmeal.

muzzle The area round a horse's mouth.

native pony A breed such as Exmoor, Welsh or Highland that was bred on the moors and mountains of Britain.

near side The left side of a horse or pony.

neck strap A strap that passes around a horse's neck either a) for a rider to hold on to, or b) part of a **martingale** or **breastplate**.

neck-reining A way of turning used in Western riding in which both reins are held in one hand.

Norfolk Trotter A fast-trotting harness horse that existed between the 15th and mid-20th centuries; ancestor of the Hackney and others.

noseband The part of a bridle that goes round a horse's or pony's nose.

novice An inexperienced rider or horse.

numnah A saddle-shaped pad used under a saddle to prevent it from rubbing and to absorb the horse's sweat.

off side The right side of a horse or pony.

on the bit A horse's head held in the position in which the rider has the maximum control of him.

outline The shape a horse's or pony's body makes when he is being ridden.

overface To ask a horse to do work, such as jumping, which is beyond his current stage of training.

pace a) Another word for **gait**. b) A specific gait in which a horse moves both legs on one side together.

pack pony A pony that carries heavy loads in packs that are strapped to its back.

part-bred A horse or pony that has one **pure-bred** parent, or two pure-bred parents of different breeds.

part-coloured When a horse is more than one colour, such as skewbald.

pastern The part of a horse's leg between the foot and the **fetlock** joint.

pedigree A table that lists an animal's parents, grandparents, great-grandparents and so on.

pelham A type of **bit** with two reins and a curb chain.

plain head An unattractive or ugly head.

poached ground Ground that is cut up and muddy.

point of the shoulder The front of the shoulder joint, where the shoulder blade joins the first bone of the animal's foreleg.

points a) The physical features of a horse. b) Areas on a horse that are described as part of its colour. A horse with 'black points' (usually a bay or a dun) has a black mane, tail and lower legs.

pommel The front part of a saddle.

pony An equine animal which stands up to 14.2 **hands** (147cm) high.

pony-like head A small, neat head with small ears and large eyes.

port A raised, half-moon shape in the mouthpiece of a **curb bit** that allows room for the horse's tongue.

presence The way that a horse or pony carries itself.

primitive When it is used to describe a breed, 'primitive' means at an early stage of evolution.

pulling a mane and tail Pulling out a few long hairs to tidy up a mane and tail.

pure-bred A horse or pony that has two parents of the same breed **registered** in the breed's **stud book**.

putting to Harnessing a horse to a vehicle.

quarter marks Decorative patterns made on the **quarters** by brushing against the lie of the coat with a damp brush.

quartering A quick brushing over done before exercising a horse or pony.

quarters The area of a horse behind the saddle – his hindquarters and hindlegs.

quick-release knot A knot used to tie up a horse and a haynet. Pulling the end of the rope releases the knot instantly.

quiet Said of a calm horse that is not easily upset.

rack A fast **pace** in which each foot hits the ground separately.

ragwort A yellow-flowered plant that is highly poisonous to horses and other animals.

registered Listed in the **stud book** of the breed to which the horse or pony belongs. A registered horse has a **pedigree**.

rein back Stepping backwards. The horse's legs move in **diagonal** pairs.

reins The parts of a bridle that run from the **bit** to the rider's **hands**.

rhythm The evenness and regularity of the horse's or pony's hoof beats.

roller A broad band that fastens round a horse's belly to hold a rug in place.

Roman nose A nose that, seen in profile, is convex, or curving outwards.

running out When a horse or pony refuses to jump a fence by going round the side of it.

safety harness The adjustable straps that hold a riding hat in position.

safety tabard A vest worn over riding clothes to warn motorists of the rider's presence or that the horse is nervous or inexperienced.

school a) A riding arena. b) To exercise a horse for its education and training.

schooling Training a horse.

seat a) A rider's position in the saddle. b) The part of the saddle on which a rider sits.

showing Exhibiting a horse or pony at a horse show, where it is judged on its **conformation** and **paces**.

showjumping A jumping competition at a horse show.

shying Jumping sideways when startled.

side reins Reins that run from the **bit** to a **roller**.

skipping out Collecting droppings from a stable in a basket or skip.

skull cap A hard, brimless hat used for riding.

sloping shoulders Shoulders that slope from the **withers** to the **point of the shoulder**. They give smooth, comfortable **paces** in a riding horse.

sluggish Said of a lazy pony that is reluctant to work.

snaffle bit A **bit** that is usually jointed in the centre and has two rings.

solid colour The same colour all over, with markings on the legs and face only.

sound A 'sound' horse is a healthy one, with no lameness or breathing problems.

Spanish Horse The most important European breed of horse for centuries, which had a huge impact on horse breeding throughout the world. Most American breeds are descended from the Spanish Horse.

spread fence A wide fence with the back part higher than the front.

stable stains Marks on a stabled horse caused by lying in dirty bedding.

stallion A male horse or pony, aged four years or more, used for breeding.

stamina The ability to keep going even when very tired.

straight action Moving the legs straight forwards and backwards without any sideways movement.

strapping Thorough grooming of a stabled horse, done after exercise.

stride The distance travelled by a horse's foot between two successive impacts with the ground.

stud book A book in which the name, date of birth and **pedigree** of a **pure-bred** horse or pony is **registered**, or listed. Every horse and pony breed has a stud book.

studs Metal pieces screwed into the heels of a horse's shoes to prevent it slipping.

surcingle A strap attached to a rug to fasten it round a horse's belly.

suspension The moment in canter when all the horse's feet are off the ground at the same time.

sweat scraper Used for removing water from the horse's coat when washing it or sponging it down.

tack All the pieces of saddlery used on a riding horse or pony.

take-off The stage of a jump when a horse launches itself into the air.

temperament A horse's or pony's nature, for example, calm, gentle or excitable.

thatching Putting straw under a wet horse's rug to help it dry without getting the rug wet.

Thoroughbred A breed of horse registered in the General Stud Book. All racehorses are **registered** Thoroughbreds.

throatlash The part of a bridle that goes under the horse's throat and stops the bridle from slipping forwards.

top line The upper part of a horse's back, from the **withers** to the hindquarters.

topping a field Cutting down weeds and long, coarse grasses to improve grazing.

trace Part of driving **harness**; a strap that pulls the vehicle. It runs from the collar hames to the vehicle.

transition The change from one **pace** to another. An upward transition is from a slower to a faster pace; a downward transition is from a faster to a slower pace.

tree The framework on which a saddle is built.

trotting poles Poles laid on the ground for training a horse or rider to jump.

tug A leather loop through which the shaft of a vehicle passes. Tugs prevent it from tipping up or down.

turn out a) To let a horse loose in a field. b) A vehicle pulled by a horse or pony.

under saddle When a horse or pony is ridden.

up to weight Capable of carrying a heavy rider.

upright shoulders Shoulders that do not slope very much from the **withers** to the **point of the shoulder**. They are better for carrying a **harness** collar.

vaulting a) Jumping up on to a horse without using the stirrups. b) Gymnastics on horseback.

waist The narrowest part of a saddle's **seat**.

water brush A short-bristled brush used damp to lay the mane and tail in place when grooming.

weighband A tape wrapped round a horse's **girth** from which you can read off its weight.

whip a) A device used to urge on a horse. b) The person who drives a horse.

wind A horse's breathing.

wings The sides of a jump.

withers The bony ridge at the base of a horse's neck.

worming Giving medicine to kill parasitic worms inside a horse's intestines.

zebra marks Horizontal dark stripes on the legs of **primitive** breeds of ponies.

Index

A

action 12, 24, 31, 32, 46, 48, 50, 54, 55, 62, 64, 69, 71, 189, 190–191, 198, 202–203, 216
age 8, 9
ageing 9, 16
aids 132, 149, 156–171, 174–177, 183–188, 190, 201, 208, 210–211, 216
ailments 122–123
Akhal-Teké 29
albino 16, 17
allergies 75, 95, 117, 122
American barns 78, 216
American Saddlebred 54
American Shetland 66, 67
Andalucian 48
Anglo-Arab 21, 28, 39
anti-cast roller 107
Appaloosa 17, 53, 67
approach 184–185, 216
Arab 24–25, 26, 28, 29, 31, 32, 39, 41, 56, 58, 59, 60, 61, 68, 69, 70, 193
Ardennais 31, 37
Asiatic Horse
    see Przewalski's Horse
Assateague 68
Australian pony 70
Australian Stock Horse
    see Waler

B

backing 209, 216
balance 132, 158–161, 165–168, 175–177, 184–185, 188–189, 198, 208, 216
bandages 109, 112–113, 120–121
Barb 29, 31, 47, 56, 59, 68, 69
Basuto 56, 69
bedding 75, 81–83
behaviour 12, 89, 118, 122, 148–149, 157, 202
Belgian Heavy Draught
    see Brabant

biting 7
bits 10, 134, 136–137, 139, 140–141, 144–145, 153–154, 161–162, 165, 188, 206, 208, 212, 216
    'on the bit' 161, 188
blaze 18, 216
blinkers 212
bloodstock 26
body brush 97, 98–99, 216
body language 6
body protector 130, 197, 216
Boer 69
Boerperd
    see Boer
bone 12, 28, 39, 40, 56, 59, 216
boots 112, 128, 130–131, 156
bot-flies 122
Boulonnais 31
bounce fence 216
Brabant 20, 36
breaking in 208–209
breast collar 212
breastplate 216
breathing problems 76, 95, 117
breeching 213, 216
breeching strap 113, 210, 216
breed society 216
bridles 125, 128, 134, 136–137, 138–139, 140–141, 142, 144–145, 208, 212
bridleways 182, 183
bridoon 137, 216
browband 137, 139, 140, 144–145, 212, 216
bucket muzzle 95
bucking 216
buckjumping 56
bulk feeds 77, 91, 92
Byerley Turk 26

C

Camargue 43
cannon bone 15, 216

canter 166–167, 174, 177, 182, 185, 189, 191, 198, 202, 208
cantle 135, 138, 151, 216
carriage 47, 207
carriage horse 12, 32, 37, 40, 41, 42, 47, 66
Caspian 68
catching a pony 76, 88–89
cattle 73, 87, 183
cavalry horse 10, 39, 41, 48, 56, 214
cave paintings 10, 44
chaff 93, 216
changing the rein 175, 216
chaps 111, 131, 216
chariot 10
chariot racing 10
cheekpieces 136–137, 139, 142, 144, 145, 216
Chincoteague 68
cinch 138–139, 216
circulation 74, 109
clean-legged 32, 33, 216
clenches 100, 110–111, 216
clenching tongs 111
Cleveland Bay 42, 47
clipping 104–105, 106, 115, 120, 216
clothing (riding) 130–131
Clydesdale 18, 35, 36, 62
coach 212, 213
coarse mix 93, 216
coat 98, 102, 104–105, 117, 195
cob 12, 13, 216
cob-sized 136
coldblood horses 20, 21, 30–37
colic 75, 93, 122–123, 216
collar 210, 211, 212, 216
collected paces 190–191
collecting ring 200
collection 190–191, 216
colours 16–17
colt 216
companionship 6, 73, 74, 124–125
competing 192–193, 196–205
competition horse 38, 39, 40–41, 59, 216

competitions 129, 185, 192, 196–205, 211
concentrates 92–93, 216
conformation 12, 14, 27, 202, 216
Connemara 59
contact 154–155, 156–157, 160–161, 165, 166–167, 170–171, 216
convalescence 124
coughs 76, 117
crest 15, 216
Criollo 50
cross-bred ponies 133
cross-country 39, 41, 46, 47, 204–205, 216
croup 14, 216
curb bit 137, 139, 216
curry combs 97–99, 216
cuts 109, 120

D

Dales 62
dandy brush 97, 98–99, 216
Darley Arabian 26
Dartmoor 58
deep litter 82, 217
deep through the girth 82, 217
dehydration 117
diagonals 164–165, 175, 217
diet 90–95
digestive system 15, 87, 91
dished face 24, 217
dishing 217
dismounting 152–153, 183, 198
disunited 167, 217
DIY livery 217
dock 14, 97, 99, 217
domestication 5, 6, 10, 11, 74, 148
double bridle 137, 217
draught horse 12, 30–37, 46, 217
drawing knives 111
dressage 5, 28, 29, 39, 40, 41, 42, 48, 127, 156, 157, 174, 188–189, 190–191, 192, 194, 202–203, 205, 217
driving 12, 37, 42, 46, 47, 48, 60, 61, 62, 64, 66, 71, 206, 207, 210, 211, 212–213

driving bridle 212
dropped noseband 217
droppings 82, 85, 86, 117
drum horse 214
Dutch Draught 37
Dutch Warmblood 40–41

E

ears 6, 15, 66, 109, 117, 123, 140, 145
eel stripe 19, 45, 50, 63, 64, 217
endurance riding 24, 25, 28, 29, 69, 193
equus caballus 5
eventing 5, 27, 28, 29, 39, 40, 41, 204–205, 217
events 127, 129, 185, 192–193, 196–205
evolution 5
exercise 74, 91, 103, 106, 109, 110, 117, 125
exercises 174–175, 178–179
Exmoor 5, 58
extended paces 190–191
extension 190–191, 217
eyes 14, 15, 17, 53, 58, 97, 99, 114, 117

F

Falabella 70
farm horses 10, 30, 31, 32–36, 40, 42, 46, 50–51, 61, 62, 63, 64–65, 69
farriers 100, 110–111
feather 30, 31, 33, 34, 36, 37, 57, 61, 62, 217
feet 5, 17, 19, 29, 30, 41, 50, 51, 52, 53, 54, 63, 76, 87, 97, 100–101, 108, 109, 110, 111, 115, 117, 121, 123, 140, 184, 191, 194–195
Fell 62, 71
fences 184–185, 186, 187, 200–201, 204–205
fencing 84–85, 88
fender 138, 217
fetlock 14, 18, 19, 195, 217
field shelters 74, 79, 84, 217
fields 74–79, 84–88, 95, 106, 114–115, 117, 123, 125, 129, 149, 168, 204

fighting 7
filly 217
first aid 112, 120–121
five-gaited horses 54, 69
Fjord 19, 64, 217
flat work 186, 217
flehmen reaction 6
flesh marks 18
flies 74, 114, 120, 122
flying change 166, 191, 217
foal 7, 8, 9, 207, 209, 217
food and feeding 5, 6, 33, 71, 74–75, 77, 81, 90–95, 109, 112, 115, 124, 129
foot care 100–101, 109, 110–111, 115, 121, 194–195
forehand 188, 217
forelock 15, 144, 217
forges 110, 111
forward position 168–169, 184–185, 217
four-beat pace 54, 169, 217
French Trotter 39, 43
Friesian 37, 62
frog 100, 217
full livery 217

G

gaited horses 54–55, 64, 69
gaits 54–55, 64, 69, 157, 160–161, 164–169, 171, 176–177, 182, 189, 190–191, 202, 217
gallop 117, 127, 168–169, 182, 184, 198
games, mounted 198
gamgee 120–121, 217
gates 84–85, 88, 183, 200
Gelderlander 40, 42
gelding 217
gig 212, 213, 217
girths 106, 109, 135, 137, 138, 141, 142–143, 147, 155, 157, 161–163, 165–166, 189, 212, 217
gloves 128, 130
Godolphin Arabian 26
going 217
grass livery 217
grazing 5, 6, 20, 43, 58, 71, 73–74, 84–87, 91, 95, 117, 125, 196

grazing rotation 87, 217
Groningen 40
grooming 6, 77, 79, 96–99, 108, 109, 124, 142, 194
gymkhanas 127, 180, 192, 198–199, 217

H

hack 12
hackamore 139, 217
hacking 127, 165, 173, 180, 182–183
Hackney Horse 46, 71
Hackney Pony 66, 71
Haflinger 36, 65
half chaps 131
half-bred ponies 133, 217
half-pass 191
halt 152, 160–161, 163, 170–171, 188, 202
halter breaking 209
hames 212
hand signals 181
hands 154, 156, 159, 161, 162-163, 170, 181, 211, 217
Hanoverian 39, 40, 41
hard feed 77, 91–93, 115, 217
harness 206, 210, 212, 217
harrowing 86
hats 128, 130, 131
hay 75, 77, 79, 81, 90–91, 92–93, 95, 112, 115, 124
haylage 217
haynets 77, 81, 92, 95, 105, 109, 112, 124
headcollars 88–89, 95, 98, 114, 136, 140, 142, 144, 159, 209
headpiece 136–137, 139, 142, 144–145, 217
headstall 139
health 74, 94, 116–125
heavyweight riding horse 12, 21, 35, 42, 46
herding 51, 56, 60, 62, 69
herds 5, 6–7, 148, 149
Highland pony 19, 63, 94
hock boots 112
hogging 13, 217
holidays 127, 180
Holstein 40, 41

hoof 17, 19, 100, 110, 111
see also feet
hoof cutters 110–111
hoof oil 97, 101
hoof pick 97, 100–101
hoof testers 123
horn (saddle) 138, 151, 170
horse trials 205
horseboxes 112–113, 196
hosing 102–103, 120, 123
hotblood horses 21, 23–29
Household Cavalry 214
hunter 21, 46, 217
hunter trials 127, 192, 204
hunting cap 130–131, 217
hyracotherium (*Eohippus*) 5

I

Icelandic 21, 64
impulsion 165, 184, 217
in hand 119, 202, 217
inbred 217
indoor schools 129, 147
infections 120, 121, 123
in-foal 8
instinct 5, 148
instructors 128, 146–147, 158–159, 177, 184
internal organs 15
intestines 15, 91
Irish Draught 46

J

jodhpurs 130
jog 171, 217
joints 15, 24, 27, 94, 112
jousting 11
jump off 200, 217
jumping 5, 29, 39, 41, 53, 56, 59, 60, 130, 135, 184–185, 186–187, 192, 197, 200–201, 204–205
jumps 184–185, 200, 204

K

keeper 145, 217
kicking 7
King's Troop, Royal Horse Artillery 215
knee 15, 218
kneecaps 112

L

lameness 87, 100, 118–119, 122, 123
laminae 100
laminitis 94–95, 100, 122–123, 218
landing 185, 218
lateral 218
lateral work 188, 191
leading 88, 89, 109, 125, 128, 130, 136, 142, 147, 148, 153, 158–159, 177, 184, 196, 209
leading file 218
leading leg 166–167, 189, 191, 218
leading rein 147, 158, 159, 177, 184
'leg into hand' 157, 218
leg up 150, 218
leg yield 188
levade 49
ligaments 123
light-reflective equipment 182
liming field 86
Lipizzaner 49
litter 87
Liverpool bit 212, 218
livery 78, 218
loading 113, 218
long-distance riding 28, 29, 193
long-reining 206–209, 218
loose boxes 78, 81, 128, 218
loose rein 109, 156
lunge cavesson 208
lungeing 74, 130, 158–159, 176–177, 208, 218
Lusitano 48

M

mail coach 11
mane combs 97
manège 218
mangers 81, 91
mare 8, 218
markings 16, 17, 18–19, 33, 35, 45, 52, 53, 62, 63, 64, 67, 218
martingales 136–137, 140, 218
mealy-coloured 58, 218

measuring stick 132
medicines 124
medium walk 157
merychippus 5
mesohippus 5
mineral licks 93
Missouri Foxtrotter 55
Morgan 50
mounting 147, 150–151, 198
mounting block 150
muck heaps 81, 83
mucking out 75, 77, 81, 83, 142
mud fever 115, 123
muscles 15, 74, 109, 208
Musical Drive 215
Mustang 56
muzzle 15, 218

N

nail pullers 111
nails (horseshoe) 110–111
native ponies 115, 218
near side 218
neck straps 137, 158–159, 177, 218
neck-reining 170–171, 218
New Forest pony 59
Norfolk Roadster 42
Norfolk Trotter 43, 46, 55, 218
Noriker 36
nosebands 136–137, 139, 140, 142, 144–145, 208, 218
novice 218
numnahs 141, 143, 218

O

off side 218
Oldenburg 42
outdoor schools 129, 147
outline 218

P

pacing 55, 64, 67
pack pony 62, 64, 218
Palomino 52, 65
part-bred 218
pastern 12, 14, 19, 218
pedigree 218
pelham 137, 218

Percheron 32
piebald 17, 52, 68
pincers 110–111
Pinto 52
plain head 40, 42, 55, 68, 218
plaiting 194–195
planning permission 78
pliohippus 5
ploughing matches 34, 35
poached ground 85, 218
point of the shoulder 15, 218
points 218
points of a horse 14–15
poisonous plants 84, 85, 86
police horse 5, 214, 215
polo ponies 13, 50
pommel 135, 141, 142, 152, 153, 218
pony breeds 20, 21, 57–71
pony clubs 180
Pony of the Americas 67
poultices 120–121
presence 24, 218
primitive breeds 19, 44–45, 64, 218
pritchel 111
Przewalski's Horse 4, 19, 44–45, 64
pulse 118
pure-bred ponies 133, 218
putting to 210, 218

Q

Quarter Horse 51, 53
quarter marks 195, 218
quartering 77, 99, 218
quarters 179, 218
quick-release knots 92, 142, 218

R

racing 10, 24, 25, 26, 27, 29, 39, 43, 51, 55, 69
rack 54, 69, 218
ragwort 84, 86, 218
rasp 111, 119
refusal 185, 187, 200–201, 204
reins 109, 136–137, 138–139, 142, 145, 147–148, 150–163, 165–167, 168–169,

170–171, 175–178, 181, 183, 184–185, 188, 202, 206, 208–209, 210, 211, 212, 213, 219
respiration 117, 118
rhythm 167, 219
riding 12, 26, 27, 39, 42, 46, 54, 55, 56, 59, 60, 61, 62, 64, 65, 69, 76, 79, 100, 109, 115, 126–129, 146–147, 154–193, 198, 200–205
riding clothes 130–131, 203
riding holidays 127
riding schools 128–129, 150
riding, classical art of 49, 190
'Ring of Fire' 215
rising trot 164–165, 184
road safety 181
Rocky Mountain Pony 66, 67
rodeos 56
rollers 106, 107, 208, 219
rolling (field) 86, (horses) 107, 123
Roman nose 29, 34, 45, 46, 47, 48, 49, 50, 56, 219
rosette 196, 212
roundings 137
rugs 81, 99, 103, 104, 106–107, 109, 112, 115, 124
running out 185, 219

S

saddle blankets 138–139
saddle soap 112, 141
saddles 134–135, 138–139, 140–141, 142–143, 150–151, 153, 154–155, 158–159, 162, 164–167, 168, 170, 176–179, 184, 189, 202, 208, 209, 212
safety harnesses 130–131, 219
safety tabards 182, 219
schooling 186, 188, 198, 219
schools (arenas) 172–175
scurry driving 71, 211

seat 154–155, 162, 165, 166, 168, 169, 170, 176–177, 178, 184–185, 219
Selle Français 39
senses 6
shafts 210
sheep 73, 87
Shetland 66, 70, 71, 211
Shire 34–35, 36, 213
shoeing 54, 100, 108, 110–111
shortening the reins 154
shoulder-in 188
showing 5, 12, 25, 27, 35, 37, 46, 51, 52, 54, 55, 63, 66, 70, 71, 156, 192, 194, 196, 197, 202, 219
showjumping 27, 28, 29, 39, 40, 41, 42, 186, 187, 200–201, 205, 219
shying 149, 219
side reins 208, 219
side-saddle 189
sitting trot 165
skeleton (horse) 15
skewbald 17, 52, 68
skipping out 82, 219
skull caps 130–131
sliding halt 51
sloping shoulders 12, 219
slow gait 54, 69
sluggish 219
snaffle bit 136–137, 140, 208, 219
solid colour 219
soundness 219
snip 19
sock 18
Spanish Horse 46, 47, 48, 50, 52, 53, 56, 59, 61, 219
Spanish Riding School of Vienna 49
Spanish trot 11
Spanish walk 48
sponges and sponging 97, 99, 102–103, 109, 112, 141
spread fence 200, 219
spurs 156
stable rubbers 97, 99
stable stains 97, 219
stables 73–83, 93, 104, 106, 109, 114, 115, 122, 124–125, 128

stallion 7, 26, 66, 219
stamina 24, 27, 28, 29, 43, 50, 53, 55, 71, 193, 219
Standardbred 55
star 19
starvation paddocks 95
steeplechasing 27, 205
stirrups 134, 138, 141, 142, 147, 150–155, 164, 170, 176–177, 178, 184, 189, 209
stocking 18
stomach 15, 91, 122
straight action 202, 219
strapping 219
stride 165, 186–187, 190–191, 200, 219
stripe 19
stud book 66, 219
stud farm 26, 58, 59
Suffolk 33, 36
summer 74, 76, 87, 114, 122–123
sunburn 114
supplements 93
surcingle 106, 107, 219
suspension 166, 219
sweat scraper 102, 219
Swedish Warmblood 39
sweet itch 122
swellings 109, 119–123

T
tack 76, 109, 112, 128, 134–145, 147, 154–155, 203, 208, 219
tack rooms 128
tacking up 138–139, 141–145
tail bandaging 112–113
take-off 185, 219
tandem 212
Tarpan 44, 45
teeth 6, 8, 10, 94, 119
temperament 33, 36, 37, 40, 42, 50, 51, 65, 219
temperature 118–119
Tennessee Walking Horse 54
thatching 109, 219
Thoroughbred 12, 26–27, 28, 35, 39, 40, 41, 42, 43, 46, 50, 55, 56, 58, 59, 69, 70, 94, 133, 219

throatlash 136, 144–145, 219
titbits 73, 88, 89, 93, 124, 148
top line 219
topping (field) 85, 87, 219
toys 124
trace 210, 212, 219
trace hooks 210
trail riding 55, 61
trailers 112–113, 196–197
training 5, 206, 207, 208–209, 214–215
Trakehner 39, 40, 41
trandem 213
transitions 161, 165, 219
travelling 106, 108, 112–113, 196
tree (saddle) 136, 219
trekking 61, 62, 63, 64, 65, 69, 127
tripod 111
trot 37, 43, 46, 55, 61, 64, 71, 164–166, 171, 174–177, 184–185, 190, 202–203
trotting poles 184–185, 219
tubbing foot 121
tugs 210, 219
turning 162–163, 170–171, 177, 181, 188, 190, 211
turn on the forehand 188
turn on the haunches 190
turning out a pony 81, 88–89, 219
tying up 81, 113, 136, 140, 142, 197
types of horse/pony 12–13, 132–133

U
under saddle 219
up to weight 219
upright (straight) shoulders 12, 219

V
vaccinations 118
vaulting 193, 198, 219

vets 14, 119, 120, 123–125

W
waist (of saddle) 135, 150, 219
Waler 56
walk 157, 158–159, 160–161, 165, 171, 175–177, 183, 184–185, 190–191, 202
wall eyes 17
warmblood horses 21, 38–56
washing 102–103, 194
water 74, 77, 81, 82–83, 84–85, 91, 109, 112, 114, 115, 124
water brush 97, 99, 101, 219
water, riding through 183
weighbands 94, 219
weight (horses) 94, 95
Welsh Cob 59, 60, 61, 62
Welsh Mountain Pony 58, 60, 70
Welsh Pony 60, 61, 71
Welsh Pony of Cob Type 61
Western riding 127, 131, 151, 170–171
Western shows 50, 51, 52
Western tack 138–139
whips 149, 152, 156–157, 165, 189, 211, 219
wind 219
wings of jump 185, 219
winter 104, 106, 114–115, 123
withers 15, 132, 141, 143, 150, 152, 159, 164, 176, 219
working canter 167
worming 118–119, 219
worms 85, 86, 87, 94, 117–119

Y
Yorkshire Roadster 46
Yorkshire Trotter 71

Z
zebra marks 19, 45, 63, 64, 219

HORSE AND PONY WEBSITES

www.bef.org.uk
British Equestrian Organization

www.bhs.org.uk
The official British Horse Society site

www.equestrian.org
The American horse shows
association – USA equestrian

www.equiworld.net
International horse and pony
information

www.horsesport.org
Fédération Equestre Internationale –
International Federation of
Equestrian Sport

www.horseworlddata.com
General horse and pony information
for enthusiasts

www.ilph.org
International League for the
Protection of Horses

www.imh.org
International Museum of Horses

www.pony-club.org.uk
The official Pony Club site

www.hartpury.ac.uk
Information on courses run and
events held at the centre

www.talland.net
Information about the school and
the courses run there

www.horselink.co.uk
Links for the top horse and pony
care and riding websites

www.newrider.com
Advice and information
for keen new riders

www.swhp.co.uk
Society for the Welfare of Horses
and Ponies

NOTE TO READERS

The website addresses listed in this
book are correct at the time of
going to print. However, due to the
ever-changing nature of the internet,
website addresses and content can
change. Websites can contain links
that are unsuitable for children. The
publisher cannot be held responsible
for changes in website addresses or
content, or for information obtained
through third-party websites. We
strongly advise that internet searches
should be supervised by an adult.

ACKNOWLEDGEMENTS

Kingfisher would like to thank:
Inspector Alan Hiscox of the
Metropolitan Police
Dickie Waygood, Riding Master of
the Household Cavalry
Captain Mark Dollar of the
Household Cavalry.

Everybody at **The Talland School of
Equitation**, especially the Hutton
family and Patricia Curtis.

Everybody at **Hartpury College
Equestrian Centre**, especially
Margaret Linington-Payne.

Models:
Tom Alexander
Alison Jane Berman
Anna Bird
Emily Brady
Blake Christian
James Cole
Emily Coles
Patricia Curtis
Wesley Davis
Sam Drinkwater
Parker Dunn
Amelia Ebanks
Naomi Ebanks
Theo Freyne
Helen Grundy
Sarah Grundy
Simon Grundy
Emma Harford
Brian Hutton
Charlie Hutton
Pippa Hutton
Hannah James
Pete Jenkins (equine dentist)
Olivia Kuropatwa
Sophie Kuropatwa
Eric Lin
Margaret Linington-Payne
Rhiannon Linington-Payne
Ella McEwan
Thomas McEwen
Lucy Miller (advanced riding)
Charlotte Nagle
Alasdair Nicol
Gemma Oakley
Andrew Poynton (farrier)
Jay Rathore
Nicola Ridley
Ignacio Romero Torres
Ros Sheppard (Western riding
consultant)
Victoria Taylor
Max Thomas (farrier)
Sophie Thomas
Camilla Tracey
Ayako Watanabe
Laura Wilks
Sawako Yoshii

Additional photography by:
Art Archive p10bl, p10c, p10/11t,
p10/11b, p11tr; Houghtons Horses
p31br, p32b, p37tl, p46bl, p50br,
p54bl, p56br, p56bl, p61c, p69tr;
Only Horses Picture Library p36bl,
p43b, p45bl, p65b; Sandy
Felsenthal/CORBIS p214/215b